Fat chance!

Why do so many people spend their lives dieting? Would life *really* be wonderful if only you were thinner? *Fat Chance!* investigates the myths behind dieting and explores how they are created and perpetuated by an ever-growing dieting industry, which says that if you feel fat you must be fat.

Jane Ogden uses her experience as a young woman growing up in a weight-obsessed world, together with her own psychological research, to challenge the powerful money-making industry of the dieting world. She shows how the process of dieting itself sets you up for failure – by making you think about food, dieting means you see food as something special, encouraging you to eat more not less. *Fat Chance!* offers an alternative to dieting, not a magic pill for weight loss, but a way to stop building the dieting industry and a way to feel good about yourself. By helping you understand dieting, the book frees you from the feelings of guilt, self-dislike and failure, which are central to the dieter's world.

Fat Chance! opens our eyes to the reasons why we feel fat. It will be a compelling read for anyone who has ever felt fat, been on a diet, or shared their life with a dieter.

Fat chance!

The myth of dieting explained

Jane Ogden

London and New York

First published in 1992
by Routledge
11 New Fetter Lane, London EC4P 4EE

Simultaneously published in the USA and Canada
by Routledge
a division of Routledge, Chapman and Hall Inc.
29 West 35th Street, New York, NY 10001

© 1992 Jane Ogden

Typeset in Palatino by LaserScript Limited, Mitcham, Surrey

Printed and bound in Great Britain by
Biddles Ltd, Guildford and King's Lynn

British Library Cataloguing in Publication Data

A catalogue record for this book is available from the British Library.

Library of Congress Cataloging in Publication Data

Ogden, Jane, 1966–
Fat chance : the myth of dieting explained / by Jane Ogden.
p. cm.
1. Reducing. 2. Reducing diets. 3. Reducing—Psychological
aspects. 4. Women—Health and hygiene. 5. Body image.
I. Title.
RM222.2.035   1992
613.2'5—dc20   91–44109
                                                         CIP

ISBN 0–415–07371–5

Contents

Acknowledgements

I would like to thank Bernadette Duffy, Jackie Ganley, David Marks, Andrew Lownie and my family for their valuable comments, criticisms and suggestions on earlier drafts. I am also grateful to Dr Tim Roper at Sussex University for encouraging me to follow a career in research and to Dr Jane Wardle for supervising my PhD which prompted this book. Also I thank everyone who has been willing to discuss food, women and dieting at great length whenever I felt the need. I would also like to thank Robert for supporting me both financially and emotionally whilst I was writing this book.

I am also indebted to all the women and men who took part in my various studies and who were prepared to talk openly and honestly to me.

Introduction

When I was twelve, we used to play 'blockee', off-ground touch, knock-down ginger and chase. I used to wear my sister's cast-offs, eat what was put in front of me and when I was hungry. When I was fourteen, I discovered boys! I used to hang around in the local record shop for the latest focus of my affections, and force my friends to walk endlessly around school in the hope of spotting talent.

And suddenly everyone was dieting. Instead of the usual doughnut at break, there was an apple, and a lunch of fish, peas and chips was replaced by a salad sandwich, carefully spread with low calorie, low taste margarine. Some dieted to follow their older sisters, some felt forced to by the fright of encroaching puberty, others simply joined in with everyone else.

Food developed a special role. It was no longer something to stop hunger, it became a focus, an interest and a treat.

At home, my mum always had the up-to-date slimming magazines and the latest meal-substitute. Women's magazines were full of diet sheets and lists of good and bad foods. I can remember a feature on how many uncooked versus cooked mushrooms you can eat for 1000 calories – 20 pounds of them! – with photographs of mounds of raw vegetables. Everyone seemed to be dieting. Everyone seemed to count calories, watch the scales and read the bumf.

Yet no-one ever got any thinner. For all this effort no-one really lost weight. My friends bounded through adolescence developing all the appropriate female hips, thighs and bottoms, and my mum continued to weigh the same as she had always done.

So what were they actually doing? What was going wrong? The diet books say 'eat less and you will lose weight'. These women seemed to eat less, at least they talked and read about it enough, but with no weight change.

Through the course of my work as a psychology researcher, I got into an interesting conversation with a 40-year-old woman. She was married with two children, very attractive, lively and a perpetual dieter.

How long have you been dieting?
Oh, probably since I was about 20, I suppose – twenty years.
What do you weigh now?
About 10½ stone.
What do you want to weigh?
About 9½ stone.
What did you weigh when you started dieting?
About 9½ stone.
She started to giggle. Why do I bother?

This woman had been thinking about dieting, trying to eat less, buying separate food, not going out for dinners and spending a fortune on the latest slimming ideas for the last twenty years. She was your average woman. Not obese, not even overweight, just heavier than she wanted to be. And she was a dieter. Yet she had never really lost weight; in fact, since she had started to diet she had gained a stone.

Up to 90 per cent of the female population diet at some time in their lives. Very few lose weight and even fewer maintain any weight loss. What is happening? Why do so many woman diet and yet not lose weight? Why do they diet in the first place and why do they continue? What is so great about being thinner, and why do so many women feel fat?

These are the questions I aim to answer.

A multitude of myths surround dieters and dieting behaviour. We believe fat people eat differently from thin people, that dieters are fat and that dieting is the solution to being fat. We believe that failed dieters are weak-willed and that all you have to do is eat less.

These are the myths I wish to dispel.

Most women diet because they feel fat, not because they are unhealthily overweight. Being severely overweight can have negative effects on your health. Perceiving yourself as overweight can also have negative effects on health because it motivates dieting behaviour. Constantly attempting to diet can increase depression and feelings of inadequacy, and also decrease your metabolic rate. Dieting is the problem, not weight.

It is necessary to evaluate why you are dieting.

Being thin is associated with success, attractiveness, sexuality and self-control. Are you dieting to achieve these goals? If so, challenge them directly, not by trying to lose weight. Thin people are not happier than their larger counterparts, nor are they more in control of their lives. The dieting companies make a profit out of women's feelings of inadequacy and promote the idea that dieting will make you thinner and more content with your life.

For the large majority of women, dieting does not work. Dieting creates more problems than it solves; dieting and overeating become a vicious circle. Dieters never stop dieting, and never stop using the dieting industry.

This book is aimed at the average-sized woman who is led to believe that she is over-sized. It does not offer a new way to lose weight or a magic recipe for thinness, but questions why women, whom everyone else sees as being thin, want to be thinner. The dieting world is a powerful money-making industry, and most authors shy away from questioning the very root of its success: the belief that being thinner is better and that dieting is **the** way to achieve this goal. This book aims to challenge these beliefs and illustrates that they are based on myths which are both created and perpetuated by the industry which benefits from their existence.

Understanding dieting frees us from the feelings of guilt and self-dislike which are central to the dieter's world. Psychological research offers an understandable explanation of why diets fail, and takes the responsibility away from the personal weakness of the failed dieter. This book explains diet breaking in terms of the many factors intrinsic to the dieting process. If you don't lose weight, you are not weak-willed but are responding to the many changes which are created by trying to diet.

Giving up dieting is a rewarding experience. It opens the door to renewed self-confidence, self-esteem and acceptance and rids us of the need constantly to criticise ourselves as we are now by comparison with an elusive future self.

Chapter 1

Taming the female form

Putting dieting into perspective

For as long as records have been kept and history has been written the female body has been seen as something to control and master. Whether it was in the form of Chinese foot-binding, female circumcision, the wearing of corsets or bustles, women's bodies have been viewed with an eye to changing them. Feet, breasts, waists, thighs and bottoms have been either too large or too small according to the fashion of the day. Padding was needed to add size or binding used to reduce. No aspect of the female body has ever been accepted simply as it is.

And dieting is the modern-day equivalent. As women, we regard our bodies with a critical eye, we examine every inch from the size of our nose to the hair on our toes to see if it is acceptable. And now we want to be thinner. To understand the late twentieth century's obsession with dieting it is necessary to understand the history behind the powerful need to tame the female form.

We have a basic understanding of the terms masculine and feminine. Although men and women may vary over the years, fashions may change and economic climates alter, some things remain the same. Men are larger than women. They are taller, wider, have larger feet and broader waists. To tame the female body has often meant to emphasise these differences.

CHINESE FOOT-BINDING

An old Chinese saying states:

> If you care for a son, you don't go easy on his studies;
> If you care for a daughter, you don't go easy on her foot-binding. (Ts'ai-fei lu)

Women tend to have smaller feet than men. And the Chinese tradition of foot-binding emphasised this difference. A central part of Chinese life for about a thousand years, it began to die out only at the beginning of the twentieth century with the Kuomintang encouraging the 'letting out of feet'.

The process

Young girls had their feet bound at about the age of seven. The mutilation process was carried out by the girl's mother and other close female relatives who would bind each foot so that the large toe pointed upwards and the other toes were tightly bound under the foot. The young girl would then be made to walk and put her weight onto the newly bound foot; the bones would break and the structure of the foot would be rearranged to conform to the 'lotus hook' shape.

The result

After what was obviously an excruciating process, the young girl would be left with painful three-inch long 'hooks' or stumps which meant that the girl could not run, had to hobble when she walked or even had to be carried.

Why foot-binding?

A foot-bound woman was marriageable material. 'Lotus hooks' were regarded as objects of desire and seduction by men, one of whom has been quoted saying:

> the lotus has special seductive characteristics and is an instrument for arousing desire. Who cannot resist the fascination and bewilderment of playing with and holding in his palms a soft and jade-like hook?

The lotus hooks also symbolised obedience and that your wife would be incapable of running away. The stumps prevented women from any independent life of their own and represented total helplessness and reliance on male power. Perhaps the most interesting element of foot-binding is that women did it to women. It was a tradition for women, executed by women. However, even though women were the mutilators, the goal of acceptability to men was an essential element of economic security and social status. The women were prepared to suffer and to pass this suffering on through their family as a sign that they understood and respected male ideas of beauty, and out of fear of being unmarriageable.

In the western world we tend to regard mutilations such as foot-binding as horrific and alien to our cultural standards. However, is it that different from our own traditions?

CORSETS

Women have smaller waists than men. The corset emphasises this difference.

The corset has played a major role in the world of female fashions. Although an apparently familiar and harmless article it has possibly been responsible for more fainting fits, more crushed ribs and more wasting muscles than any other form of bodily control.

The need for corsets was derived from the idea that women were insufficiently strong to support their own weight. It was believed that the female waist and spine were too weak to support the breasts and stomach. Of course the corset had many other uses. It created an upright, 'regal' appearance and emphasised the feminine smaller waist. As fashions changed, the corset provided a basis to enlarge or flatten the stomach and to round or flatten the bottom. Women wearing corsets were incapable of bending and so needed to be waited on, and, constantly breathless, they required a male arm to steady them. In fact, the corset played a central part in creating the very weakness for which it was designed to compensate.

And the main message of the corset: 'I am prepared to change my body and suffer pain in order to be of marriageable material.' Moulding your body to create the ideal form suggests an acceptance of women's role in society and an understanding of the necessary means to become desirable. It suggests a recognition of the objectification of women and the central role that physical attractiveness plays in determining their identity. Of course, men may also use equivalent beauty aids, but men in corsets, built-up shoes or toupees are laughed at. As Susan Brownmiller says in her book *Femininity*, such men:

have been grist for the jokester's mill, under the masculine theory that real men do not trick themselves out to be pleasing. (They have better ways to prove their worth.) A woman on the other hand is expected to depend on tricks and suffering to prove her feminine nature.

The corset represented women's need to be a desirable object to the men who could provide the necessary social acceptability.

BREAST-BINDING

Breasts have always been another problem area. Whether they should be large, small, droopy or firm has been left to the ever-changing whims of the fashion world and the male appreciators. I don't think that any other part of the body has received so much attention, so much criticism and so much obsessive fixation as the female breast.

The symbolism of the breast is obvious. It denotes sexuality, fertility and motherhood. It is also a constant reminder that we are animals and possess 'udders' in the same way as cows and mammary glands in the same way as all other mammals. Yet the association between breasts and their biological function is constantly denied. Large breasts are hoisted up, pointed out or flattened down, whilst flat-chested women pad their breasts out. But we all fear the biological destiny of our breasts. As Susan Brownmiller says in *Femininity*:

> we have seen too many pictures in *National Geographic* of wizened old females with sagging, shrivelled teats or with udder-like breasts that hang forlornly to the waist. No not sexy. Not pretty and attractive. Entirely too remindful of the she-animal function.

We have detached our breasts from their biological function and hoisted them into the realms of a fashion accessory. Fashion dictates their acceptability.

In the 1920s women bound their breasts tightly to create the flat-chested, boyish flapper look. In the 1950s Marilyn Monroe and Jane Russell rendered the flat-chested look unattractive and women wore padded, underwired, push-up bras to make the most of whatever they had. The 1970s meant that bras were out but only small breasts could survive the lack of support and the 1980s brought larger breasts back into fashion again.

Western women have bound their waists and breasts in the same way that Chinese girls had their feet bound. Women conform to contemporary ideas of femininity to increase their marriageability and gain economic and social stability. There are physical differences between men and women, and women are taught a variety of tricks, mutilations and tortures to emphasise these differences and thus emphasise their femininity. If femaleness is defined as the opposite to maleness, then to be more different from men is to be more female.

FREEDOM

And then there was freedom. Women traded in their corsets for rubber roll-ons and traded in their roll-ons for freedom. Boudicca-like bras were exchanged for the softer, lighter versions which were in turn exchanged for the luxury of going bra-less. Women were allowed and even expected to release their bodies and to resort to the natural support of flesh and muscles. Great! At last women could accept their bodies for what they were.

And then there came the bikini and along with it Twiggy was launched enthusiastically onto the fashion scene. Suddenly, at the beginning of an era of natural control and natural support, we were told that we should not have any flesh to control or support. Bikinis gave no protection to flesh; they represented a freedom that was available only to those without any excess bodily parts. Twiggy did not need to wear a bra or corset; she had no need to squash her body in only for it to reappear elsewhere. But this absence of need did not come from a desire to free the female body, but from the very fact that she had nothing to free. Women could go bra-less as long their breasts revealed only a restrained life of their own, and corsets were out, as long as what was left behind did not need a corset.

For centuries whale bones, latex, nylon and cotton had been used to reshape and rearrange any aspect of the body which did not conform. Even in the 1920s' thin 'flapper' days, bras and corsets were an acceptable way to control the female form. But now we are free from these artificial devices.

And are left with only our flesh to control.

The messages are the same. Breasts, bottoms, thighs, stomachs should be rounded or flat as determined by the whims of the fashion world. But to comply we have to change our actual bodies.

And this is where dieting raised its ugly head.

Weight Watchers started in America in 1963 and came to Britain in 1967. And the first copy of the first *Slimming* magazine was issued in 1969. The 1960s represented the onset of the dieting boom.

Chapter 2

Who is dieting?

People who are fat eat differently from those who are thin.
Dieters are fat, which is why they try to lose weight.
This is what we are told.

DO FAT PEOPLE EAT DIFFERENTLY?

Imagine seeing a thin person on a train eating a chocolate bar.
What do you think? Probably very little. Thin people can eat high
calorie food without others really noticing or drawing major
conclusions about their eating behaviour. Now imagine seeing a
fat person doing the same. It is a completely different issue.
'Probably their fifth today', 'that's why they are fat' and 'some
people have no control' are common responses. It is assumed that
fat people are fat because they eat differently than their thin
counterparts. It is assumed that they have no control over their
food intake and that they overeat.

Several studies were carried out in the 1960s and 1970s to
evaluate the power of these prejudices towards fat people. In 1969
Maddox and Liederman asked a group of physicians and medical
students to rate their fat patients for a set of personal characteristics. They found that 97 per cent judged them stupid, 90 per
cent unsuccessful, 90 per cent weak, 86 per cent lazy, 69 per cent
not nice, 65 per cent unhappy, 60 per cent weak-willed, 54 per
cent ugly and 55 per cent awkward. In a further study in 1979,
Larkin and Pines found that fat men and women were less likely
to be recommended for employment by college students who
watched them performing tasks in an identical fashion to their
thinner counterparts.

Research has also evaluated how young we are when we learn

these prejudices. In 1969 Dr Lerner showed groups of 5- and 10-year-old children drawings of different sized adults. The adults were either thin, medium or fat. The children were then asked to describe what kind of person the adult would be. The children associated the medium-sized adults with all the positive qualities and the thin and fat adults with all the negative qualities. In a further experiment the researchers presented the children with five drawings of children: handicapped child; facially disfigured child; child with crutches and leg brace; child with amputation of left forearm; and obese child. The children were then asked 'tell me which boy (girl) you like the best'. All the children rated the obese child as the one they liked *least*. The researchers concluded that this was because obesity was seen as the fault of the child and not something to be sympathised with. The children saw obesity as resulting from being greedy, weak and lazy. The prejudices against fat people are strong in adults. But they also seem to be just as powerful in children. To what extent are these beliefs based on fact?

Because of the belief that overweight people are in some way different from thinner people, research has attempted to find differences in personality between the two groups. Studies have looked at differences in depression, neuroticism, self-control and many other personality traits. The results suggest that, although some fat people are depressed, some are neurotic and show poor self-control, so do some thin people, and that there are no overall differences between fatties and thinnies. The fat personality is often believed to be 'jolly'. It is often suggested that if you are overweight you have to be 'jolly' to compensate. The research suggests that there is no evidence for this myth.

What else do we believe about fat people?

Perhaps the strongest myth which surrounds the issue of size is that fat people overeat. The idea of fatness raises questions as to what causes it. Is fatness due to environmental factors or is it a product of the individual's genetic make-up?

Fatness runs in the family. The probability that a child will be overweight is a direct product of their parents' weight. Fat parents have a 40 per cent chance of producing fat children. The probability that thin parents will produce fat children is very small, about 7 per cent. However, parents and children share both environment and genetic constitution, so this likeness could be due to either factor.

Couples who live together for a long time tend to grow fatter or thinner together. Their environment is similar so their sizes become similar, suggesting that genetic factors are secondary. However, recently there has been mounting evidence to suggest that genetics are the main determinant of weight. Twin studies involve examining the weight of identical twins reared apart, who have identical genes but different environments. Studies also examine the weights of non-identical twins reared together, who have different genes but similar environments. The results show that the identical twins reared apart are more similar in weight than the non-identical twins reared together. Genetics seem to play a vital role in determining fat.

More convincing are studies using adoptees, which compare their weight with that of both their adoptive parents and their natural parents. Stunkard, in 1986, found a clear relationship between adoptees' weight and that of their natural parents, and no relationship between their weight and their adoptive parents'.

So, if genetics are important, some people are born to be fat and others are born to be thin. However, environment must still be important. Whatever your genetic constitution, food needs to be available to put on the weight in the first place. And this raises the vital question of whether fat people are fat because they eat more of this food than thin people.

Food intake can be measured either in the laboratory or using more natural methods. One way to measure food intake is to use a controlled experimental environment. The subject is asked to have lunch or to take part in an experiment which supposedly has nothing to do with food, such as watching a film, and then the experimenter measures how much she eats. Either food can be casually placed next to the subject or she can be asked to rate snack foods for their taste and quality. Using these methods there has been no evidence to support the prediction that fat people eat more than thin people. Some fat people eat a lot but then so do some thin people. The amount eaten seems to be determined by the individual, not by their weight.

The problems with these kinds of study are numerous. People are affected by the sterility of the environment and are always aware of being watched. More natural studies try to overcome these problems.

Experimenters have evaluated the amounts that both fat and thin people eat using such techniques as watching them in bars, restaurants and canteens, seeing how much they eat and examining who prefers what kind of food. At least twenty studies have been published looking at eating in the environment, and the results suggest that there are no clear-cut differences between the ways fat people and thin people eat, nor any difference in what they eat. It would seem that both thinnies and fatties like sweet foods, both like high calorie foods and both eat the same amounts.

However, it could still be argued that fat people eat more in the privacy of their own homes than thin people. To test this Coates and his colleagues, in 1978, went into the homes of sixty middle-class families to examine what was stored in their cupboards. They weighed all members of the families and found no relationship between size and shopping. Being fatter does not mean that you eat more at home.

A common belief is that if you look into a fat person's shopping trolley at the check-out you will find sweets, crisps and biscuits. It is believed that a fat person will chose high calorie food in a restaurant and that they are fat because they stuff themselves with chocolate. These studies suggest that these are just some of the many myths surrounding fat people. Fat people may eat chocolate, but so do thin people. We all know of someone who has 'hollow legs' and can eat as much as they like. Fat people do not eat more food than, or different food from, thin people; they are simply predetermined to use this food differently and to store it as fat.

So where does this myth come from?

At the beginning of this century, being large was a sign of health and being thin was a sign of malnutrition. Being fat suggested that you had enough money to buy food, and thinness meant you didn't. Nowadays, it is assumed in the western world that everyone has access to the appropriate amounts of food. Therefore, to explain why some people are larger than others, size is regarded as being directly related to how much you eat of this food.

The dieting industry thrives on this belief. Rosemary Conley's *Complete Hip and Thigh Diet* has sold a million copies to date. It offers a way to shed 'those inches other diets leave behind'. And it associates being fat with overeating. She writes 'Bingeing is, I believe, the greatest cause of overweight' (p.25). The evidence suggests that this is not the case. Some overweight people binge and so do some thin people. Overweight seems to be caused by your genetic constitution, not bingeing. Obviously you need to eat to become overweight, but you do not need to binge.

Rosemary Conley also describes in detail what kind of foods overweight people eat. She writes that overweight people must have eaten:

> too many fatty and sugary foods which are positively loaded with calories – bread spread with lashings of butter, an abundance of fried foods, cream cakes, biscuits, chocolates, crisps and so on. The types of foods overweight people love. (p.65)

Do overweight people love these types of food? Probably some do, but so do some thin people as well. It is assumed that overweight people eat more and differently than their thin counterparts and that this is why they are overweight.

In *The Beverly Hills Diet* (1980), Judy Mazel writes:

> It is imperative that you exercise control when you eat combinations. Don't let your heart take over. Eat like a human being, not a fat person.

She believes that fat people eat differently than thin people. She suggests that they are out of control and eat for emotional reasons and not because of hunger.

Susie Orbach's *Fat is a Feminist Issue* revolutionised women's attitudes towards food and weight. It brought eating problems out into the open and provided a framework for discussion. However, Susie Orbach also directly associates weight with an underlying psychological problem. She states that:

> Fat is not about lack of self control or willpower. Fat is about protection, sex nurturance, mothering, strength and assertion. Fat is a social disease. (p. 28)

She too believes that being fat is a sign that you have a problem with eating. Orbach calls fatness a disease as she believes that people have become fat as a response to social pressures and a need for protection from the outside world. Conley believes that you are fat because you overeat, and Orbach believes that you overeat to create a barrier between you and the world.

Why does 'fat' have to be to do with anything other than being fat? Why does it have to be indicative of any psychological problem? What is wrong with believing that you are fat because you were born this way? Some fat people have eating problems, and some have other psychological problems. But not all, and no more than thin people do. Being fat is being above the average weight. If you are above average height, do you also have a problem? If you have larger than average feet (a personal interest!) are there underlying psychological reasons?

Dr Kelly Brownell is an expert on obesity and said in 1987:

> The recognition of the role of genetics has expanded society's view of obesity, so that psychological problems are no longer inferred simply because an individual is overweight.

He believes that we have got to the stage where size is understood in terms of genetic predisposition, and not in terms of a problem with food. Yet this optimistic view is somewhat premature. However often we are told that genetics determine size, we are also told twice as often that fatness is an indication of an underlying problem. Weight has taken on a special meaning, and this special meaning is initiated and perpetuated by a growing industry.

So why does the dieting industry promote this myth? If your weight means nothing other than that you are overweight then you do not require any help. If your weight means that you have an eating problem, then this automatically puts you in a position where you need help. It defines you as inadequate and out of control and therefore creates an opening for someone to provide this help. This is where the dieting industry comes in. It offers help to all those 'fat people who cannot manage on their own'. It is necessary for the dieting industry to sell the idea that fat means a problem so that they can go about solving this problem. However, it is a problem that they themselves have created.

WHY ARE SOME PEOPLE FAT?

So why are some people fat? If fat people do not eat more or differently than their thinner counterparts, and obesity can be explained in terms of their genetic constitution, how does this genetic tendency express itself? The research into the effects of a genetic predisposition to obesity has looked at both metabolic rate and the number of fat cells an individual has. Both these perspectives throw some light onto the situation, but neither has resulted in any clear-cut conclusion.

Metabolic rate theory

The body uses energy for exercise and physical activity, but also for carrying out all the chemical and biological processes which are essential to being alive. The rate of this energy use is called the metabolic rate and it has been argued that obese people have lower metabolic rates than average weight individuals. People with lower metabolic rates burn up less calories when they are resting and therefore require less food intake to carry on living.

Recent research in America evaluated the relationship between metabolic rate and weight gain. A group of scientists in Phoenix assessed the metabolic rates of 126 Pima Indians by monitoring their breathing for a forty-minute period. The study was carried out using Pima Indians because they have an abnormally high rate of obesity – about 80 to 85 per cent – and were considered an interesting group. The subjects remained still and the levels of oxygen consumed and carbon dioxide produced were measured. The researchers then followed any changes in weight and metabolic rate for a four-year period and found that the people who gained a substantial amount of weight were the ones with the lowest metabolic rates at the beginning of the study. In a further study, ninety-five subjects spent twenty-four hours in a respiratory chamber and the amount of energy used was measured. The subjects were all followed up two years later and the researchers found that those who had originally shown a low level of energy use were four times more likely to show also a substantial weight increase.

These results seem to suggest a relationship between metabolic rate and the tendency to weight gain. If this is the case then it is possible that the same individuals are predisposed to become obese because they require fewer calories to survive than their thinner counterparts. However, in direct contrast to this prediction there is no evidence to suggest that obese people generally have lower metabolic rates than their thinner counterparts. In fact research suggests that fat people tend to have slightly higher metabolic rates than thin people of similar height. So what do all these contradictory findings mean? One interesting point which could explain these results is that weight gain can actually cause an increase in metabolic rate. In fact in the study described above, the Pima Indians who gained weight also showed an increase in their metabolic rate, to such an extent that it became equal to that of the Indians who had a faster rate to start off with. It is possible that individuals with slow metabolic rates have a tendency to gain weight, but that once they have gained this weight their metabolic rate increases to match the rate of individuals who are not prone to weight increases. Therefore the reason why the obese have the same metabolic rates as thin people could be that they have gained weight which has resulted in a corresponding increased metabolic rate. However, research has not yet shown this to be the case.

Fat cell theory

Another theory which has been presented to explain the size differences between people has suggested that the obese may have more fat cells than other individuals. The number of fat cells is largely determined by genetic factors. However, when the existing number of cells has been used up, new fat cells are formed from pre-existing 'preadipocytes'. Most of this growth in the number of cells occurs during gestation and early childhood and remains stable once adulthood has been reached. It could be suggested that overfeeding a baby could result in obesity when the child grows up; however, the research seems to suggest that this is not the case. Although the results from studies in this area are unclear, it would seem that, if an individual is born with more fat cells, then there are more cells immediately available to fill up. It is possible that the genetic tendency for obesity expresses itself in a larger number of fat cells which are easily filled up with fat. One thing which is clear as far as this area of research is concerned is that once fat cells have been made they can never be lost. An obese person with a large number of fat cells may be able to empty these cells but will never be able to get rid of them.

We are told, and we believe, that fat people have a problem and eat more and differently than thin people. The dieting industry promotes this problem so that it can then offer to solve it. The research suggests that fat people are genetically predisposed to gain weight, and that their weight is not a product of overeating. However, it is still unclear how this genetic tendency is expressed.

ARE DIETERS FAT?

Imagine going to dinner at the house of a male friend. You arrive and his wife is still upstairs getting ready. You look around. The book shelves are lined with *The Bum and Leg Diet*, *The Grapefruit Diet*, *The Sensible Eating Diet* and many others. Is his wife thin or fat? You probably expect a fatty to come down the stairs.

We believe: 'people diet because they are fat'. So is this true? Are dieters fatter than non-dieters?

For a start it is difficult to define what being fat is. But, accepting this for the time being (see Chapter 3), research suggests that dieters come in all shapes and sizes. Some dieters are fat, some dieters are thin. Some fat people are perfectly happy with their size and do not diet, whereas some people whom others would see as having no weight problem think they are fat and diet. Dieters all have one thing in common; they think they are fat and they diet. They see themselves as being larger than they want to be. Their actual size is immaterial, what motivates dieters to diet is their perceived size.

So where does this myth come from?

Dr Barry Lynch says 'If you feel fat your body is trying to tell you something: lose weight' – his opening line to his book *The BBC Diet*. He assumes that if you feel fat you must be fat. Most women feel fat but are not actually fat. Anorexics most certainly feel fat, but most definitely are not fat. Dr Lynch makes the mistake characteristic of the slimming industry.

Imagine waking up one morning and feeling fed-up. It is a special day and you want to look your best; however, nothing you try on looks quite right. You say to your friend 'I feel really ugly today'. She replies, 'You are ugly; have you thought of having plastic surgery?' This is what authors such as Dr Lynch do. They take people's feelings of self-dislike and self-criticism and they treat them as fact. You feel ugly therefore you are ugly, you feel fat therefore you are fat.

What is wrong with asking 'Why do I feel fat? Maybe I can get rid of this feeling.'

In his chapter 'A nation of fatties', Dr Barry Lynch writes 'A third of the population are regular users of one or more slimming products. It seems that it's the norm in this country to be overweight.' Why are users of slimming products overweight? Why should all the women who buy 'Lean Cuisine' foods and

Slimmer be overweight? Some of them probably are overweight, but many others probably just feel fat and don't like their bodies. Maybe some people buy the magazines for the recipes or for the interesting case histories. Dieters are not necessarily fat, and examining who supports the dieting industry provides no insight into who needs to lose weight. Anorexics often buy all the latest slimming aids, read all the magazines but do not illustrate that people who pay money to the industry are overweight.

The dieting industry sells itself to people who want to lose weight. It is used by women who *see* themselves as being fat, yet acts as if these women *actually are* fat. Slimming magazines do not try to 'stop you *feeling* fat', they sell various ways to 'stop you *being* fat'. Slimming aids are bought by women of all shapes and sizes, yet we are told that they 'make you thinner' not 'make you feel thinner'. The majority of dieters have a problem with feeling fat, not with being fat, but the dieting industry does not distinguish between the two. We therefore believe that dieters are fat, and dieters are reinforced in their perception of themselves.

We are sold a multitude of myths around dieting which are accepted as fact. Simply by looking around and examining our responses to different people, it soon becomes clear that we believe that fat people eat differently than thin people and that dieters are fat.

It would seem that this is not the case.

Chapter 3

Why do so many women diet?

Up to 90 per cent of women try to lose weight by dieting. Why do so many women want to be thin? What is so great about thinness? And why has dieting been offered as the solution to the fat problem?

Thinness is healthy and thinness is attractive. This is what we are told. Is this true and is the drive for weight loss as simple as this?

HEALTH AND THINNESS

Women diet because they are told and they believe that it is unhealthy to be overweight. What constitutes overweight and how overweight you have to be for it to be a health risk are questions which are not as easy to answer as we are led to believe.

The medical profession has invested a large amount of time and energy into investigating the negative effects on health of being overweight and obese. This motivation supposedly comes from their concern for the well-being of the individuals involved and yet often appears to reflect social ideas of aesthetics and attractiveness.

Being overweight constitutes weighing more than an ideal weight for the individual's height and weight. These ideals are measured according to height–weight tables developed by life insurance companies and their estimation of life expectancies. The most commonly used tables are those devised by the Metropolitan Life Insurance Company in America which analysed the longevity and weights of its policy holders. Although providing a rough idea of what is healthy, they are based on the averages of a large group of people and do not take into account individual life-styles, fat versus muscle percentages, time when weight was gained, family history and build. The tables do not state exactly how much each individual should weigh and yet are often referred to by doctors and used to back up their own personal preferences for body weight.

To provide a rougher idea of the relationship between health and weight, in 1985 a panel of experts from the National Institute of Health in America decided that a weight of 20 per cent above average constitutes a health risk and that a weight of 40 per cent more constitutes a severe health risk. However, body mass is not the only indicator of being overweight. An obese person has too much body fat; a body builder may weigh the same and yet have far less fat.

So, fat is hard to measure, and the relationship between weight and health is complex, and given that it is difficult enough to determine how much fat is acceptable, assessing the health risks is even more problematic.

Accepting these problems for the time being, what are the predicted health risks? Research suggests an association between being overweight or obesity and a number of health problems.

Hypertension

Research suggests that overweight people are 2.9 times more likely to have high blood pressure. Untreated hypertension increases the risks of heart attack, stroke and kidney disease.

Diabetes

Overweight people are more likely to develop diabetes than non-overweight people.

Coronary artery disease

Obesity can cause the narrowing of the arteries causing heart attacks and other related problems.

There are several other problems which are often associated with being obese, such as trauma on the joints, complications during pregnancy and death!

It must be pointed out that there are numerous problems with identifying the associations between weight and health. Firstly, being overweight does not necessarily cause these problems and may simply reflect other underlying problems such as lack of exercise and poor diet. Secondly, thin people also suffer from these disorders and, finally and perhaps more importantly, some overweight people diet and, as will be discussed in detail later on, this is perhaps the most dangerous risk to health and well-being of all.

However, having now probably succeeded in frightening you with the horrors of being overweight and obese, there is one final statistic that is important at this stage. About 16 per cent of the female population are obese. However, somewhere up to 90 per cent of the women in this country diet at some time in their lives. So why are all these women attempting to lose weight? Obviously some of them are doing it for health reasons, some are doing it for what they believe are health reasons; however, the rest are motivated by something else. What is it?

THINNESS AND ATTRACTIVENESS

One of the most obvious motivations for dieting is the drive to be thin and attractive to others. In *The Beverly Hills Diet*, its author Judy Mazel suggests that if someone should comment 'You're getting too thin' you should reply 'Thank you'. We should be thin and the thinner the better.

Anyone who has visited art galleries and stared up at the ceilings of cathedrals and chapels will be well aware of the large and rounded women desired by men in the seventeenth, eighteenth and nineteenth centuries. Being overweight was regarded as a sign of prosperity, of having ample food and the ideal state of female sexuality. Women are born to have thighs, hips and breasts and plumpness was an indicator of fertility and beauty. In direct contrast to this, present society presents us with an increasingly thin and decreasingly feminine role model.

As women, we are constantly told by magazines, television, films and adverts that we should be thin, and that when we are thin we will be attractive to the opposite sex. Not only are we told that we should be thin but the idea of thinness appears to be getting thinner. A study in Canada analysed the weights of Miss America Pageant contestants between the years 1959 and 1978. They found that, whilst the average weight of American women

under 30 increased by about 0.3 pound per year, the weights of
the contestants decreased at almost exactly the same rate. In
Britain, a study published in 1989 examined the physical features
of female fashion models recruited by an agency in London
which supplied models to women's magazines such as *Vogue*,
Cosmopolitan and *Woman's Own*. The researchers examined the
changes in the models' height, bust, waist and hip measurements,
and found that over the years 1967–1987 the models became progressively taller, with a decrease in hip and bust measurements
relative to waist measurement producing a more androgynous
shape.

If the shapes and sizes presented by the media illustrate
thinness, then by definition nearly all women are overweight.
The motivation to be thinner is not specific to those who are
overweight; it is general to those who perceive themselves as
being overweight. We cannot all be 16, nor can we have the body
of a 16-year-old model, and therefore if we accept the messages
sent to us we should all wish to be thinner and it would seem that
up to 90 per cent of us do.

Owing to the discrepancy between our bodies and the ideal
body, women show considerable body dissatisfaction. Women
tend to report specific repulsion at certain areas of their bodies,
and these are most commonly their thighs, hips or bottoms. In my
work as a researcher into dieting behaviour, women who were of
average weight would often say 'if only I could just cut off bits of
my thighs' or 'it would be great just to slice a bit off my bottom'.

This self-dislike is perpetuated by the language used by the
dieting industry. Phrases such as 'saddlebag hips', 'elephant
thighs', 'enormous posterior' and 'thunder thighs' are used to
describe those bits of the body which should not exist. The words
illustrate the disgust and hatred focused on the female body and
the way that we see our bodies as an enemy and repellent. This
hatred motivates us to develop our self-dislike and perpetuates
the need to get rid of such atrocities. The dieting industry does
not understand that when dieters say 'thunder thighs' it reflects
how they see their thighs, not how big their thighs actually are.
Self-criticism reflects your mood and your self-esteem. Yet the
dieting industry takes self-criticism as fact, develops it and then
offers ways to get rid of the thighs, not the perception of the
thighs.

And anyway what is wrong with having thighs, hips and a

bottom? Nothing, except women are no longer expected to have them!

Along with the discrepancy between the desired and the actual body size, women have also been found to have a distorted view of their size. It was originally believed that only women with eating disorders showed body size distortion. The original technique used to examine this distortion involved two lights mounted on a bar. The subject was asked to stand a specified distance from the bar as the experimenter turned a wheel which brought the lights either closer together or further apart. The subject was then asked to say when she felt that the lights corresponded to the width of certain parts of her body. In 1973 it was found that anorexic patients significantly overestimated their body size and believed that their hips, shoulders and waists were larger than they actually were. More recent studies have shown that *all* women regardless of actual weight overestimate their body size by up to 10 per cent, that is, they perceive their bodies as being larger than they actually are.

Not only does society tell us that as women we should be thinner than we are, but in addition we perceive ourselves as being fatter than we actually are.

We are presented with the problem that we are overweight, but what else are these messages actually saying?

The obvious message which comes from all this pressure is thinness is attractive and 'be thin and you will get a man'. The images tell us that thinness is attractive and, specifically, attractive to the object of our desires.

In a study in 1988, researchers examined the body image, attitudes to weight and perception of figure preferences in the opposite sex in men and women of two generations. The subjects were asked to examine a series of silhouettes of increasingly large bodies and to rate their ideal shape, their current shape, the most attractive shape and the shape which they believed to be the most attractive to the opposite sex. The women were categorised as mothers and daughters, and the men as fathers and sons. The results showed that all subjects except the sons felt that their current shape was larger than their ideal shape, supporting the idea that women of any age feel that they are overweight, and that young men are inclined to feel that their body-size is acceptable. Interestingly, the results also showed that women of both generations believed that men of their own generation preferred women to be slimmer than these men actually did. This suggests that women are led to expect men to like women thinner than they actually do. Perhaps the media present images which represent women's idea of the male preference and not actually the male preference.

IS THINNESS SIMPLY TO DO WITH ATTRACTIVENESS?

On the surface thinness means being able to fit into this year's latest fashions. The sale of dieting aids and attendance at weight loss clinics increase as summer arrives and women anticipate swimming costumes and shorts on the beach. As women, in a society where our worth is very much determined by our physical attributes, we are firstly something to look at and only secondly a person. We learn to evaluate ourselves in the way that others evaluate us. We learn to derive a feeling of self-worth and self-esteem from how others assess our attractiveness. A criticism of our looks can undermine our belief in ourselves as valuable human beings. As John Berger says in *Ways of Seeing*: 'Men act. Women appear. Men look at women. Women watch themselves being looked at.' We see ourselves as a reflection of how others see us.

The drive to be thin is in part motivated by a desire to be physically attractive, but maybe the reason why thinness has such a powerful hold on society is that it offers a possible means to attain all the other qualities which have come to be associated with it.

So what is so compelling about thinness?

Thinness means success. If you are thin then you will get a good job, you will climb the social ladder and you will have economic power. The woman shown driving off to the office in an expensive car, organising meetings and reaping the rewards of success is thin. Success shows the ability to dictate the future. Women still exist in a world where decisions are made for them and their options are limited. Women find themselves in situations where society sees their sex first and denies them the opportunities open to men, and thinness is offered as a means to achieve success.

Thinness means control. Thinness suggests control over food, control over work and control over life. It suggests the ability to resist temptation and control undesirable impulses. Women are brought up to live for others. They are encouraged to be the nurturers, the carers, to listen to problems and to give love to others. Self-indulgence is presented as a weakness and self-denial as the goal. Thinness is offered as a means to regain control.

Thinness means love. If you are thin you will be loved and protected. You will be loved because you are attractive and you will be protected because thinness is childlike, and the smaller amount of space you occupy the more care and protection you will receive.

Thinness means being psychologically stable. If you are fat you need to be protected from the outside world. Fatness provides a barrier and a place to hide from your problems. Thinness means you no longer need to distance yourself from others. Susie Orbach's book *Fat is a Feminist Issue* opened the eyes of the world to the associations between weight and sex. However, the book is subtitled 'How to lose weight permanently without dieting' and the aim is still presented as losing weight and being thin. Orbach presents fatness as a 'social disease' and believes that once you have discovered how your fat works for you and have come to terms with the fear of being thin you will lose weight. The book starts off by saying 'non-dieting and self acceptance might be the key to weight loss' (p.12). Thinness is still the goal, and fatness the problem. Although Orbach does not support the dieting industry, the underlying goal is the same – weight loss. And the message is the same – thinness means being stable.

Thinness, attractiveness, control, success and stability are all tied up together. To be successful you need to be thin and to be in control you need to be stable. It is a form of generalisation and stereotyping. We are presented images in the form of stereotypes, and we understand both ourselves and others according to these images. Unrelated characteristics have become closely associated and have become a powerful part of the set of expectations that we have about ourselves and others.

So why do we use these stereotypes? And why are thinness and attractiveness so important?

Imagine sitting on a train with nothing to do. You look around and sitting opposite is a young woman reading her book. You watch her. Within about five minutes you probably will have decided what she does, what she is like, whether she is happy or not, whether she is married, whether you would like her and details right down to the type of house she lives in and the colour of her wallpaper! We are capable of forming a detailed and complex characterisation of someone with only the minimal amount of information. All we know are facts such as sex, height, weight and type of clothes and yet we extrapolate from these to create a complete picture for ourselves.

In order to understand how and why this happens social psychologists have developed a theory called the implicit personality theory. This states that we all have some idea of which factors go together and which factors do not. It says that even the smallest amount of information about someone will generate a picture of what they are like because we will associate the known qualities with other unknown qualities. In 1974 Landy and Sigall carried out a series of experiments to assess this theory. One such study involved presenting male subjects with a set of essays to mark. The essays were supposedly written by the woman whose photograph was attached to it, which had previously been rated as either attractive or unattractive. The male subjects rated the quality of the essays. The results showed that the marks were highly influenced by the attractiveness of the supposed author. The more attractive 'authors' received a higher grade irrespective of the standard of their essay. The researchers concluded that the male subjects possessed an implicit personality theory, and believed that attractiveness was associated with intellectual ability. The known quality was attractiveness and they associated this with the unknown quality: intelligence.

So how does this relate to thinness?

One of the reasons why thinness is so powerful is that it is associated with attractiveness and attractiveness is associated with a multitude of other positive qualities. Every time we meet someone for the first time, or see someone across a room, we do not have the time or the capacity to find out exactly what they are like, but we are curious to develop some kind of characterisation of them. To do this we use our stereotypes and our implicit personality theory. We generalise from specific information to general information. We associate physical and visible attributes with underlying psychological attributes, because the physical information is easily available. We can see that someone is thin, they are therefore attractive and so we associate this with numerous other qualities. And we do this to ourselves. We want to be thin so that others will associate this with all the other positive qualities.

Thinness is presented by social pressures as the way to be attractive, and yet along with this message comes a complete package of other associated qualities and desirable attributes. The problem is being overweight, the goal is to be thin and we are told that the solution is to diet.

THE DRIVE FOR THINNESS AND DIETING

Dieting and thinness have become inextricably linked. The dieting industry has monopolised the motivation for weight loss. Weight Watchers, slimming magazines and slimming aids provide us with the chance to lose weight, whilst at the same time telling us to be thin. They have created and are using the same market. The industry thrives on an obsession and a motivation which it perpetuates.

So how did dieting and thinness become synonymous?

The dieting industry survives on the idea that if you are overweight, you must overeat, not just in relation to what your own body needs, but in relation to other people. It supports the idea that overweight people have no self-control and are incapable of denying themselves the pleasure of eating. The structure of weight loss clinics involves cheering on those who have managed to lose weight and reprimanding those who have not. One clinic used to punish the non-losers by putting them into a pen wearing a pig's mask! An extreme example, but not all that different from the humiliation of lining up to be weighed, having your weight read out to a group of strangers and being told to try harder and that you are obviously weak-willed.

Dieting has been sold as the solution to the need to be thin. We are told that if you diet you will lose weight. If you don't lose weight then you are not dieting properly, you have no self-control and you are inadequate. Eat less and you will weigh less. But is it as simple as this?

Women want to be thin. Fat is associated with bad health, and yet those who diet are not necessarily fat – they perceive themselves as fat. The ideal shape which is presented to us is so far below the average shape that most women are left with feeling fat and a desire to be thinner. Thinness means attractiveness, but it is also sold alongside success, control and love. The power of thinness stems from the life-style which is associated with thinness. And dieting has been presented as the solution.

Chapter 4

What are dieters doing?

Dieting involves eating less. Dieting means following a diet sheet. Dieting means losing weight. If you don't eat less, you are not dieting. This is what we believe. Imagine going out for dinner with a friend who is a perpetual dieter. You sit there and watch her munch her way through a starter, main course and a sweet followed by after dinner mints. 'She's stopped dieting', you think. 'She has decided to accept herself as she is.' We assume that to be a dieter means to eat less, but what exactly are dieters doing? Do dieters eat less than non-dieters?

WHAT ARE DIETERS DOING?

Dieting aims to decrease food intake. However, whether dieters eat less than non-dieters is disputable. Researchers have developed different ways to measure food intake which is obviously a complex issue. Laboratory studies involve giving people a selection of food and offering them a free lunch, and more naturalistic approaches involve asking people to complete diet sheets each day to provide a record of how much they eat in their normal environment. Both methods are problematic and yet provide some insight into eating behaviour.

Several studies suggest that dieters consume fewer calories than non-dieters in the laboratory. Thompson and his colleagues in 1988 used a precisely controlled environment and measured food intake in a meal which consisted of a variety of sandwiches and biscuits. The results showed that the dieters ate fewer calories than the non-dieters. In another study, Kirkley, Burge and Ammerman (1988) assessed the eating style of fifty women using four-day dietary self-monitoring forms. The women completed questions relating to time of eating and description and quantity of food intake. The results suggest that using this natural design the dieters were also found to consume fewer calories than the non-dieters. Recent research has attempted to describe the food intake of dieters in greater detail. Laessle and his colleagues in 1989 assessed food intake using a food diary over seven days. They found that the dieters tended to consume around 400 kcal less than the non-dieters, with the dieters specifically avoiding food high in carbohydrates and fat.

Even though these studies suggest that in certain conditions dieters may eat less than non-dieters, there are several problems about using experiments to understand dieters' general eating behaviour. For example, women may eat differently in the laboratory than in their home setting, and it is very likely that filling in forms about your lunch and dinner would spoil the spontaneity and pleasure of eating and probably affect the amount consumed.

However, in certain situations dieters have also been shown to eat more than non-dieters. In 1988, Wardle and Beales assessed the eating behaviour of dieters in the laboratory. Over a period of time, the dieters lost weight, suggesting that their overall daily calorie intake was less than that of the non-dieters. However, in the laboratory the dieters tended to eat more.

So, it seems that it is difficult to assess how much dieters are actually eating. In some situations they seem to eat less than non-dieters and in some situations they seem to eat more. Dieters seem to fluctuate between episodes of under- and overeating.

Although it is interesting to compare dieters with non-dieters, dieting aims to reduce your own food intake, and so it is more important whether, as a dieter, you eat less than you would do if you were not dieting at all. So, do dieters eat less when on a diet?

It is very difficult to evaluate whether dieting makes dieters eat less. To do this you would need to examine a group of women before any of them dieted, and then follow them up when some of them had started to diet. This has not been done. Alternatively, you could ask a group of perpetual dieters not to diet for a couple of weeks. I tried this and found that most of the dieters did not really know what 'not dieting' meant. They had been dieting for so many years that counting calories and watching their food intake had become a way of life – so much so that they were not really aware that they were doing it. When asked not to diet they found that they carried on dieting without realising it.

Another way to look at whether dieters are eating less than if they were not dieting is to examine weight changes. Taking into account the changes in metabolic rate (as discussed in Chapter 6) most dieters never really show any weight loss.

This lack of weight loss, together with dieters' inability to 'not diet', seems to suggest that dieting is predominantly a state of mind. It suggests that dieters think about eating less, and aim to eat less, but that these thoughts do not necessarily manifest themselves in a behaviour change. Some dieters may lose weight and some may eat less overall, but most simply think about it.

Dieting is a state of mind.

Dieting is something you think about as soon as you wake up, plan to do all day and plan to start again tomorrow. It is a way of life. Dieters have an identity and a challenge, and by challenging their weight they feel they are changing their lives. Dieting provides a framework for organising your day, and slimming clubs provide the support and social life which is otherwise absent.

Dieters who just think about dieting make up a large percentage of the dieting population. However, there are dieters who use more hazardous strategies for weight loss. These techniques illustrate the extreme end of the desire to be thin and are indicative of the more dangerous implications of body dissatisfaction.

SMOKING

Research in America suggests that smoking is the single greatest cause of death and disability. And yet people continue to smoke. It is well documented that smokers who quit smoking gain weight, and a large study carried out in 1975 suggested that smokers tended to weigh less than non-smokers, even if the latter had never smoked. Smoking can act as an appetite suppressant, and provides the smoker with something to do with her hands other than eat. It is difficult (though probably not impossible!) to smoke and eat at the same time. It has been suggested that a possible reason for continued smoking especially in women could be related to their fear of weight gain. Women could prefer the long-term risks of smoking to the short-term effects of weight gain.

To examine this idea, a study in 1988 gave questionnaires to 1076 people and found that 39 per cent of female smokers reported smoking as a weight loss strategy. Five per cent of women said they started smoking to lose weight, and the results showed that women were more likely than men to report that fear of weight gain prevented them from giving up smoking.

These women were not necessarily overweight and were not under any threat of the health risks of being overweight. Yet they preferred to risk their health in the long run than to put on weight. The desire to be thin outweighed the desire for longevity.

VOMITING

Vomiting for weight loss reasons is not specific to women with eating disorders. An alarming number of dieters vomit at some time in their attempts to be thin. In a recent study in America it was found that 12 per cent of women dieters vomited at some time. Another study found that 11.6 per cent of a dieting adolescent population vomited after overeating. These women would not be classified as having an eating disorder. However, they show symptoms of an eating disorder in their drive for weight loss.

Vomiting is not new. Romans used to have a 'vomitorium' so that they could eat as much as possible, vomit and then continue to eat. Dieters vomit so they do not put on weight. Vomiting can have very serious side effects. Sufferers often develop tooth decay as the stomach's digestive juices rot their teeth. They can experience deficiencies in certain minerals and feel tired and weak.

Dieters who vomit are not necessarily any heavier than those who don't. It would seem, rather, that their drive to be thinner is greater.

LAXATIVE USE

Laxative use is also not unique to women with eating disorders. In a recent study in America 6 per cent of dieting women and 6 per cent of dieting adolescents were found to use laxatives for weight control. Laxatives seem to make the dieter feel thinner as they cause dehydration and decrease water retention, but seem to have little effect on weight as most of the calories have been absorbed by the time they take effect.

VERY LOW CALORIE DIETS

Liquid protein diets first came onto the market in 1976 and 1977 and the Cambridge diet arrived in the early 1980s. Unfortunately the excitement which surrounded their release meant that their consumption was badly supervised and at least fifty-eight deaths were reported among users of liquid protein products and six deaths among users of the Cambridge diet. More recently, an article in a Scottish newspaper in 1990 reported that there are seventy-five cases pending against 'Nutri/System' in America, all of them being pursued by people complaining about the ill effects of the low calorie diet on their health. The article explains that 'the plaintiffs are each claiming a direct link between the diet and subsequent major gall bladder problems'. Apparently, seventy-three of these people have had their gall bladders removed and believe that this is a direct result of the diet.

Most of the very low calorie diets which are around now are safer than their earlier counterparts, but they can still be dangerous if used by the wrong people without adequate supervision. Dr Wadden from the University of Pennsylvania reviewed the use of these diets and suggests that there is a use for them in the case of severely obese individuals (about 50 per cent overweight). If used with adequate supervision and on the right people significant weight losses can result. However, without proper supervision, 'most patients treated by very low calorie diet alone regain weight almost as quickly as they lose it' (1990).

Are these diets, however, used only by the severely obese?

A report carried out in 1989 by Dr Pope suggested that they weren't. He says that weight loss programmes were offering very low calorie diets to people who were only just heavy enough to be considered overweight. In fact, if you examine the advertising campaigns of some of these diets it is obvious that they are aimed at the average dieter. The women used to model for the diets are a standard size 10, 16-year-old model, the same as those who model all other diets. If women who are only mildly overweight use such diets the results can be disastrous. Heart function can be affected and there can be damage to the body's other organs. The damage would be even greater for women who just think that they are fat.

It is interesting to wonder why these diets are targeted at your average dieter and not just at the severely obese. So few people are severely obese that there would be no profit from such a small sample. So many women want to be thinner that average dieters constitute a much larger population.

I interviewed a woman who had been given a very low calorie diet by her doctor. She was 50 years old, five foot three and weighed 10½ stone. Certainly not severely obese. She was determined to lose some weight, could not be bothered with long-term dieting and so felt that a short, sharp, shock treatment would be best. She was not warned about the dangers of such a low calorie diet and set off down the road to weight loss. The first week she lost eight pounds. Pretty impressive! The second week she lost five pounds. Again very impressive. The third week she was so bored with the drinks and so fed up with not eating anything that she gave up. Within three weeks she had put the weight back on.

It seems that these diets are given to people who are not severely obese. This is dangerous. However, maybe their very design stops them from being as dangerous as they could be. They are so boring that it is difficult to stick to them long enough for them to do any real harm!

DIET PILLS

In 1987 it was estimated that the National Health Service spends £4 million per year on appetite suppressant drugs. These drugs supposedly stop you from feeling hungry and help you lose weight. Originally the doctors used to prescribe amphetamines, but owingto their addictive qualities this practice was stopped. Nowadays less powerful drugs are used. However, these also have unpleasant side effects such as insomnia, dry mouth, lethargy, vomiting and headache. Their effectiveness is doubtful, but some research does suggest that, in the short term, dieters can lose more weight with drugs than with dieting alone. This is not surprising – feeling sick is probably one of the best and most obvious deterrents to eating known. But there is no evidence to suggest that they work in the long term.

Who uses diet pills?

If you are obese and your health is suffering the consequences of this excess weight, then maybe the risks of diet pills are worth it in the short term. However, diet pills are available to people of all shapes and sizes.

A *Which?* magazine survey suggested that up to a half of the women who consulted their doctors about their weight were offered drugs. Were all these women obese? A study carried out by the *Observer* suggests that they probably were not. In 1988 three journalists went along to slimming centres and asked for help in losing weight. None of them was obese, or even overweight, but they were all offered different forms of 'diet pills'. They were given no counselling and asked no questions as to why they wanted to be thinner. These drugs varied from placebos to amphetamines and were presented without any medical advice.

NHS doctors do not benefit financially from giving average weight dieters diet pills. However, it is quicker and less emotionally demanding to offer a prescription than to discuss why your patient wants to lose weight and why being thinner is so important to her. Slimming clinics *do* gain financially from diet pills. The dieter has to pay for them and the clinic can spend as little time with her as possible.

There is little evidence to suggest that diet pills work. In the short term they may increase weight loss but with upsetting side effects. In the long term there is no evidence to suggest that they have any use. For people who medically need to lose weight, maybe there is a use for them; for the majority of women who simply feel fat, they serve no function at all.

FAD DIETS

'The Beverly Hills diet', developed by Judy Mazel in 1980, is the perfect illustration of the fad diet. It exemplifies women's need for the magic recipe for thinness and also illustrates how eating disorders are envied and how extremes are regarded as far more interesting and profitable than anything in moderation.

Mazel must be the only author explicitly to admire and even recommend dieting behaviour which is founded on inducing a state of extreme fasting followed by purging. In a recent article, Wayne and Susan Wooley, two experts on obesity and eating behaviour, say that 'The Beverly Hills diet marks the first time an eating disorder – anorexia nervosa – has been marketed as a cure for obesity'.

The Beverly Hills Diet describes how Judy Mazel started dieting when she was 8 years old and how by the time she was at high school she was 'on everything: thyroid pills, diet pills, laxatives'. Mazel developed an obsession with diuretics which could determine whether she gained or lost up to ten pounds in one day. She then discovered that eating only fruit could have a very similar effect. And the all fruit diet is essentially what the Beverly Hills diet is. The diet recommends periods of starvation by eating only fruit. She advises 'Buy enough. . .five pounds of grapes on a grape day is not excessive' and boasts that 'I can peel and eat a mango while driving a standard shift car wearing a white dress'. However, these episodes of starvation exist purely to compensate for the inevitable binges. Judy Mazel is obviously in the clutches of the overwhelming desire to binge which necessitates the episodes of fasting. She says:

> I still eat a triple order of potato pancakes without choking, an entire roast beef without blinking an eye, a whole, extra-rich cheese cake without a single gasp. . .so can you.

However, to do this you require the diuretic effect of a fruit-only diet for the rest of the time:

> If you have loose bowel movements, hooray! Keep in mind that pounds leave your body in two ways – bowel movements and urination. The more time you spend on the toilet the better.

The Beverly Hills diet actively recommends an eating disorder as a cure for being overweight. It illustrates the author's envy of anorexics for their thinness and of bulimics for their methods of monitoring their weight. However, it also illustrates the author's desperation. As the Wooleys say:

> That training in anorexic psychopathology is selling so well holds a message. . . .The figures mean that women are so afraid of fat they are no longer willing to wait for a safe, scientific method of weight control. . . .The prevailing belief is that nothing is worse than being fat; that no price is too high for thinness, including health.

Fad diets such as the Beverly Hills diet are dangerous and based upon misunderstandings as to how people become overweight and how food is metabolised. Yet the book is a phenomenal seller. Women follow such diets because their desire for thinness outweighs all other concerns. Dieting has often been cited as the beginning of the downward spiral to eating disorders. The Beverly Hills diet actively recommends this route.

DIETING TO THE EXTREME

For the large majority of dieters, dieting means thinking about eating less, sometimes managing to do it, but compensating for periods of undereating with episodes of overeating. However, for a few dieting can become more than a habit. It can become a life-threatening obsession.

Anorexia nervosa

Anorexia nervosa or the 'slimming disease' has been increasingly well documented over the last few years. Most magazines feature articles on it and the academic journals have special sections to cater for the mounting interest in and concern about the disorder.

Anorexia has been described as 'a fear of fatness', 'a weight phobia' and 'an obsession with thinness'. It seems to occur mainly in young women and nearly always originates from an episode of dieting which then gets out of hand. Anorexics try to refuse any food, eating between 200 and 300 calories a day, and take vigorous exercise to avoid putting on weight. They show an intense dislike of their bodies and report seeing themselves as being a lot fatter than they actually are. The prevalence of anorexia is especially high amongst professionals such as ballet dancers, models and beauty students who have additional motivations to be thin. Most anorexics are women with the male to female ratio being about one to fifteen. However, it has recently been suggested that the number of male sufferers is on the increase. The symptoms of anorexia are very similar to those reported by perpetual dieters (see Chapter 7), but they are obviously much more extreme.

Bulimia nervosa

Bulimics also have a morbid fear of becoming fat, show an intense dislike of their bodies, but tend to be of average weight. They frequently suffer from uncontrollable urges to eat and from what has come to be called 'binge eating'. Binges vary from short episodes of overeating to prolonged episodes which can last several hours and can involve consuming up to 55,000 calories. Binges are often followed by periods of purging through either vomiting or laxative abuse. Like anorexics, most bulimics are women but their average age seems to be slightly higher. Bulimia is a very private disorder whereby the sufferer is often riddled with guilt and self-disgust. For this reason bulimics often avoid the attention of the medical profession, and can continue having a problem without any help or outside intervention. Several characteristics common to bulimics are also apparent in dieters, such as overeating and self-dislike, but they tend to be far more extreme in bulimics.

There seem to be several reasons why anorexia and bulimia have received so much attention from both the media and the medical profession. The most apparent reason is that they can both be life-threatening and cause obvious distress to the sufferer. It has also become clear over recent years that current treatment methods do not appear to be particularly successful. However, in addition to these there are other more subtle reasons.

Envy

The drive to be thin has become so powerful over the last few years that both anorexics and to a lesser extent bulimics are admired and even envied by certain sections of society. In a recent American film, a clothes shop assistant is talking to a potential buyer and says: 'My daughter can wear anything you know, she's lucky, she's anorexic.' It is a joke and it is funny, partly because it is in bad taste, but also because it reflects the way many women feel: that anorexics are 'successful dieters' and have managed to achieve what most of the female population are still trying to achieve: thinness.

Anorexics are envied for their self-control and self-denial. Bulimics are also envied. They have found a way to enable them to eat a lot without gaining weight. The perfect balance.

Media interest

This envy manifests itself in public interest. Any magazine with a new diet will sell more copies, as will one with an article on eating disorders. The drive to be thinner and to study all that is available on dieting transfers itself to a desire to read of the consequences of excessive dieting – eating disorders. Maybe reading case histories of anorexics is similar to reading case histories of 'slimmer of the year'. Or perhaps it is a consolation to think 'I may not be able to lose weight, but at least I'm not anorexic'. Although this is perhaps a rather cynical perspective on the interest surrounding eating disorders, this interest does appear to be a reflection of the media interest in how to lose weight.

An interest in extremes

Society has always been interested in extremes. You are far more likely to hear about 'depression' than about people who are 'fed-up'. Newspapers cover murder and not a wife simply being hit by her husband. Extreme cases of what we are familiar with make the headlines. It is the same with anorexia and bulimia. They are extremes and are therefore more interesting. They are dramatic and life-threatening.

But they are extremes and they are still very rare. Whereas up to 90 per cent of the female population diet, only about 1 per cent of women develop anorexia and about 2 per cent develop bulimia. These statistics may seem surprisingly low compared to those reported in books such as *Fat is a Feminist Issue* by Susie Orbach and more recently *The Beauty Myth* by Naomi Wolf which suggest much higher figures. The publicity surrounding eating disorders can lead us to believe that nearly every adolescent (especially in America) is either anorexic, bulimic or obese! However, much psychological research has been carried out to examine the prevalence of eating disorders and statistics are not always as straightforward as it is sometimes assumed.

One of the main problems in evaluating how many individuals suffer from an eating disorder is to define what constitutes a clinical problem. The term binge eating has created many problems with definition. In 1959 Albert Stunkard reported the occurrence of 'binge eating' which was defined as eating beyond the point of feeling hunger. In 1980 Dr Jane Wardle assessed the epidemiology of binge eating, defining it as 'eating lots of food even when not hungry'. The results from her study suggested that, using this definition, nearly all the subjects reported bingeing at least once a month. Susie Orbach also defines compulsive eating, using the following criteria: 'Eating when you are not physically hungry; feeling out of control around food, submerged by either dieting or gorging; spending a good deal of time thinking and worrying about food and fatness; scouring the latest diet for vital information; feeling awful about yourself as someone who is out of control; feeling awful about your body.' Definitions of bingeing can vary from eating behaviour which is characteristic of most people to pathological excess and the definition used determines how many people we see as suffering from an eating disorder.

To clarify this problem a stricter criterion has been developed. *The Diagnostic and Statistical Manual of Mental Disorders 111* (DSM 111) suggests that to be clinically diagnosed as either anorexic or bulimic the individual has to show a distinct symptomatology. Individuals may show some of these symptoms, such as weight loss or bingeing, and may be classified as having a disorder by certain authors but would not be clinically classified as such.

In addition to the problems with definition are the problems with understanding statistics. It is necessary to analyse the population used to reach a final statistic, for example, the age, sex and social class of the population will affect how the statistics should be interpreted. Comparing several studies illustrates this problem. In 1981 Halmi and her colleagues carried out a survey on American college students. They report that as many as 13 per cent showed all the symptoms necessary for a diagnosis of bulimia. However, students are a very limited group who tend to be young, white and from a high social class, all common attributes of women with eating disorders. Such statistics are worrying but are derived from a selection of the population most likely to show eating disorders. In a more recent survey Cooper and Fairburn attempted to get around this problem. In 1983 they gave questionnaires to women attending a family planning clinic in England. These women were from a variety of backgrounds and represented a good cross-section of the society. Twenty per cent said that they had experienced 'an episode of uncontrollable excessive eating' in the last two months. However, only 1.9 per cent fulfilled the criteria necessary for a diagnosis of bulimia, a much smaller percentage than is often reported. Eating disorders are distressing for the sufferers and their families but are not as common as we are often led to believe. Higher figures can be derived by using less strict definitions and by selecting specific populations. Using such figures can sensationalise a disorder which is upsetting enough as it is, and can undermine the suffering felt by the individuals who actually do suffer from an eating disorder.

One of the effects of this interest in extremes is that the excessive behaviour overshadows the importance of more moderate problems. The danger and drama associated with severe disorders trivialise the relevance of the more subtle difficulties.

Perhaps what people should be interested in are the normal average things which affect more normal average people. The drama associated with eating disorders detracts from the effects of dieting which may not be so dramatic or threatening but which have an impact on more people's lives. The effects of dieting may not be as exciting or traumatic but they are still important and deserve to be understood.

We assume that dieting means eating less and losing weight. For some dieters it does. But for the large majority dieting is a habit and a way of life. Dieters seem to fluctuate between days when they eat less and days when they eat more. Some dieters lose weight but most dieters simply seem to think about losing weight. They think about eating less but do not necessarily do so. Dieting is a state of mind and not a behaviour.

Dieters also have several other means of weight loss available to them. Smoking, vomiting, laxative use, inappropriate diets and diet pills are all available to those women who feel fat. Very low calorie diets are even specifically marketed at those women who simply feel fat.

All dieters have a common desire: to be thin. Some act on this desire in more dramatic ways than others.

Chapter 5

The dieting industry

I have frequently used the phrases 'we are told', 'we are led to believe', 'we accept' as if women are passive receivers of the information sold by the dieting industry. It is as if they have no independence and no ability to question and reject. They do. It is often implied that women are subjected to powers beyond their control. It is assumed that men dictate how women feel, think and see themselves. However, in recent years things have changed. Women can make decisions and can determine their futures within certain limitations. But they still choose to diet and to allow society to dictate what shape they should be. In order to understand why we accept so much of what we are told, it is necessary to realise quite how powerful this dieting industry is.

Books, magazines, newspaper articles, television programmes, slimming aids and exercise videos all make up the world of dieting. One of the main difficulties in assessing the power of the dieting industry is to evaluate whether the industry is responding to a need, whether it is exploiting this need or whether it creates this need.

Is the dieting industry aimed at the overweight or is it aimed at those who perceive themselves as overweight? Does the industry thrive on women's feelings of inadequacy or does it provide a service to eradicate this inadequacy?

RESPONDING TO A NEED

Slimmer magazine sold 142,000 copies between January and June in 1990. Weight Watchers UK has an average of 140,000 members.

Slimmer clubs have an average of 40,000 members. There obviously seems to be a need for these services, or at least people are responding to the provision of these services.

But what are these services actually doing?

In order for the dieting industry to be 'responding to a need' it is necessary for it to be aiming to treat a problem which already exists.

Does it treat obesity?

Obesity has long been defined as a weight problem. Being severely overweight can result in many problems such as heart failure, joint problems and high blood pressure.

Over the last twenty to thirty years doctors, psychologists, nutritionists and dietitians have developed a multitude of possible methods to treat obesity. These involve such procedures as surgery, jaw wiring, appetite suppressant drugs and psychological interventions. The most widely used programmes for weight loss involve behaviour therapy and behaviour modification, which is a well-documented approach and seems to produce relatively good results.

What is behavioural modification?

The behavioural treatment of obesity is based on changing daily habits and behaviours to reach the desired goal. The basic premise of behaviour therapy is to reward beneficial behaviours and discourage detrimental ones. However, state of the art behavioural treatment has a wider perspective and focuses on eating behaviours, social support, exercise, attitudes and nutrition. The aim is to modify the situations which promote eating and to evaluate the consequences of eating behaviour. Behaviour therapy involves specific processes which are aimed at modifying behaviour.

Self-monitoring

The client is asked to monitor when she eats, how much she eats and why she eats. This increases self-awareness so that eating cannot 'just happen', and enables her to evaluate her success and whether any changes have occurred.

Removing triggers

Clients are encouraged to remove any triggers to eat. Examples of this include storing food out of sight, eating in a limited number of places and at specific times, not in front of the television.

Reinforcement (reward)

The client can either reinforce herself or can be reinforced by other people. Often self-monitoring is a form of reward as the client can see how her weight and food intake are changing. Other rewards can involve buying new clothes or being congratulated by others.

Social support

Research suggests that support from family and friends can be important in determining the client's degree of success.

Cognitive change

More recent behavioural programmes have also included components which aim to change the client's attitudes and beliefs about foods. It is believed that the obese have negative thoughts about themselves and chastise themselves for their previous failed attempts at weight loss. Many of these thoughts reflect social attitudes to people who are overweight, such as that they are lazy, out of control and greedy. Obese women seem to take on these attitudes and this can undermine their attempts at weight loss. If they feel 'I am a lazy slob and a failure' then it is unlikely that they will succeed at losing weight. Their self-dislike can result in a self-fulfilling prophecy; they believe that they will fail, so they do fail. Behavioural programmes aim to change these attitudes and help the obese to have faith in their own ability to change things.

Another set of thought patterns which can be destructive is seen in the obese person's responses to foods. Often they will regard eating something high calorie as a complete binge, and will therefore feel critical of themselves, which can result in further eating. Behavioural programmes aim to help the client to put their eating into context and to learn to say 'I am not useless, the odd slip is inevitable and I will now return to my diet'. This eradicates an 'all or nothing response' which can often result in the client abandoning the diet.

Nutrition

In addition to advising the obese to stick to either 1200 calories (for women) or 1500 calories for men, most programmes also involve information about healthy eating and the correct constituents in a diet.

Exercise

Behavioural methods can be used to change food intake but they can also be used to increase physical activity. Women can be encouraged and rewarded for gradually increasing how much they walk, take the stairs and not the escalators and slowly become fitter.

Do clubs and magazines take the advice of behavioural modification?

There are several aspects of the behavioural modification programmes which the commercial organisations have clearly used in their structure.

Self-monitoring

Calorie counting and weight charts are both forms of self-monitoring. They enable the dieter to watch exactly what she eats and prevent casual eating. This form of behaviour modification plays an essential role in the running of slimming clubs and the structure of magazines. However, most clubs and magazines do not recommend recording where and when you ate and how you felt whilst you were doing it, probably because it is so time-consuming and requires greater dedication. These are important components as they enable the dieter to become aware of when she eats without being hungry, and whether she responds to certain moods or events by eating.

Removing triggers

Clubs often advise that you shop on a full stomach and pack food away out of sight. Dieters are also advised not to buy high calorie foods and to have plenty of vegetables and fruits to 'pick at'. These are all ways of removing triggers to eating and illustrate the use of a basic psychological principle by the commercial organisations.

Reinforcement

Reinforcement plays a central role in the running of most slimming clubs. Self-reinforcement comes from seeing your own weight decrease and the dieters are weighed and congratulated if they lose weight and given advice or even chastised if they do not. Competitions such as 'slimmer of the year' motivate the dieters to persist and reward those who do. Slimming Clubs offer a free class to those dieters who maintain their weight loss and *Slimmer* magazine will publish your weight loss story. The problem with reinforcement is the effects of punishment or the absence of a reward. Ideally the dieters should be deterred from gaining weight or failing to lose weight in order to encourage weight loss. However, a deterrent can also be humiliating and embarrassing. Clubs vary in the extent to which they punish dieters who do not lose weight. Slimmer Clubs do not read out the weight gain but tell the client that she should try harder next week. Other clubs use more extreme forms such as booing, jeering or having to stand in a group with the other 'failures'. This can be discouraging and can often result in the dieter giving up and not going back to the club again.

Social support

The main benefit of going to a slimming club as opposed to dieting on your own is the social support. Everyone has a common interest and a common goal, and it is there that dieters can find others who are also interested in how many calories there are in a sausage roll and how much you ate yesterday. Many dieters even remain members after they have reached their target weights, and although this is often from the need for a weight maintenance programme I suspect that it is also to do with friendship and something to do in the evenings.

Exercise

Over the last few years it has become apparent that the dieting industry has focused increasingly on recommending exercise as an accompaniment to dieting. Slimmer Clubs have a mild exercise session each week and even though it is unclear how much exercise can help actual weight loss, it can build self-confidence and heighten mood.

Nutrition

The dieting industry has become increasingly concerned with nutrition. Not only do magazines run features on calories but also on health and life-style.

However, there are several aspects of the recommended behavioural programmes that the industry has not included in its structure.

Thought change

It is still very much the policy of most slimming organisations to define specific foods as 'forbidden' and to tell their members to avoid them at all costs. Foods such as chocolate and chips are portrayed as evil and something which should not be included in a diet. This has the effect of making these foods more attractive, and consequently, when they are eaten, the dieter loses faith in herself and continues to eat.

Behavioural treatment programmes for obesity are the most widely used by professionals in the field. Their effects are well documented and they show a relatively good success rate. Slimming clubs and magazines have incorporated some of the behavioural theories into their structure and general running, and use these techniques to help their members lose weight. Research into weight loss has produced a package to help dieters lose weight. The commercial companies seem to listen to these research findings. However, it is important to know whether these organisations are using these methods to help the appropriate people: the obese and overweight. The dieting industry does not have any available figures on how many of their members are obese (this seems to vary from club to club), but reports from their organisers suggest that several of their members are obese, supporting the idea that the industry is responding to a need.

EXPLOITING A NEED

The average member of Weight Watchers is 2½ stone overweight. However, this number is high owing to the few obese members who push up the average. Most members have only a stone to lose. Do most of their members need to lose this weight or are they responding to media pressure to be thin?

Slimmer Clubs accept people with only a few pounds to lose. These women are encouraged to see these few pounds as a problem and something to get rid of. They are not asked why they want to be that little bit thinner.

The Cambridge diet is recommended for use by the severely overweight only, i.e. those about 50 per cent above the average weight for their height. Yet it is available to anyone who wants to lose weight – even if that person just sees themselves as fat.

Women who are not obese or even overweight also want to lose weight. They believe that if they could shed a few pounds their lives would be better and they would be happier people. These women also attend slimming clubs and read the dieting literature.

Only 16 per cent of the female population are obese. However, many more diet. If the dieting industry was aimed only at those who needed to diet for health reasons then their membership would be very small. But, by involving all those women who just want to be a few pounds lighter their membership grows enormously. And this is what they do. Not only do the magazines run articles on losing stones they also run ones which offer 'how to lose those extra pounds for summer' and 'clothes feeling tight? lose excess weight quickly and now'. Weight Watchers report that their members have been getting increasingly lighter over the last six to seven years, which suggests that this is a response to the 'desirable woman' becoming thinner. Research suggests that the general population is getting gradually heavier and yet the population who attend slimming clubs is getting lighter. A study carried out in Minneapolis in 1980 evaluated the weights and heights of those women attending slimming clubs. The results suggested that more than half of the members did not meet an objective criterion for being overweight.

How does the industry exploit this need for weight loss?

Society pressurises women to be thin and this idea of thinness is getting thinner. Most women feel fat but are not objectively overweight. They have a problem with their perceived weight and not their actual weight and yet the dieting industry treats this perception as fact. When dieters say 'I feel fat' it is translated into 'I am fat' and then the industry offers to solve the problem. The industry aims itself at women who are dissatisfied with their bodies.

Rosemary Conley's *Complete Hip and Thigh Diet* takes this extension of the dieting market to the extreme. She records numerous readers' success stories, many of which are from women who start off by saying 'Although I have never exactly been overweight' (p.35), 'As I was not really overweight or fat to start with' (p.31) and 'I could hardly be described as overweight' (p.29). These women are obviously not fat, nor do they even see themselves as being fat, but they still diet. This expands the dieting market even further and offers dieting not just to women who are objectively overweight, or even perceive themselves as fat, but to those women who don't even feel fat. This suggests that dieting can be used by everyone of whatever size to make them feel better about themselves.

I interviewed several editors of various magazines and organisers of slimming clubs and asked them whether they felt that aiming dieting at women who felt fat, or in some cases did not even see themselves as overweight, was exploitation. None wanted to be quoted directly, but all argued that it was not their place to challenge a dieter's wish to lose weight. They believed that they were respecting the individual's right to make her own decision, and argued that it was patronising to challenge this drive for thinness. On a recent television programme a representative from *What Diet and Lifestyle* magazine said 'if you are not happy with your weight we offer a way to change it'. She believed in accepting the public's decision to be 'not happy with their weight' and was responding to it. She did not challenge why so many women feel fat or whether there was an alternative cure for this feeling other than weight loss.

But maybe there are other ways of responding to this unhappiness without promoting weight loss. We are all brought up to respect other people for their attitudes and beliefs. Even if we disagree, we do not challenge or criticise a conviction, but believe that each person has the right to make their own decisions. But we tend to forget that these beliefs are a product of social pressures and expectations and are not necessarily sacred. Attitudes are changed by being challenged, and new beliefs are formed. It is not patronising to question someone's beliefs and to suggest an alternative way of looking at things.

But the dieting industry benefits from not challenging these beliefs. Recent reports show the degree to which they benefit financially from having a membership which is increased by large numbers of women who simply feel fat.

Not only does the industry respond to a need but it also exploits a need. By refusing to patronise those women who are not overweight, but feel fat, it can behave as if they have an objective weight problem. It exploits women's dissatisfaction with their bodies to widen the market and to benefit financially.

CREATING A NEED

The dieting industry creates the need for the dieting industry. It is a massive part of the media pressure which suggests and even dictates which female figure is in fashion. Slimming magazines use size 10 models to show off the latest clothes and slimming aids such as the Cambridge diet, Slendertone and diet foods are all advertised using very thin women. Magazines publish success stories of women who have lost weight which illustrate how much happier these women feel and how their lives have changed. Yet success is defined according to social expectations, not that particular individual's idea of success. Women who have dieted from 18 to 14 stone and have decided to stop do not get their pictures taken and their stories reported. Reaching the target weight is defined according to what the industry believes your ideal weight should be, not when you feel more positive about yourself. All the other readers who never manage to lose weight do not get their stories published; no weight loss is not something to be encouraged.

The dieting industry also suggests dieting as a way to change your life. The success stories, the offers of future satisfaction and the constant pairing of thinness with happiness promote the idea that thinness is happiness and dieting is the way to this happiness. It is impossible to read a slimming magazine without feeling fat and without making plans to eat less in future.

Magazines, television, films all show us how thin we should be. They use thin women to be attractive, to model their clothes and to be seduced by the male heroes. The slimming industry is part of this promotion. It is part of the creation of the need for a slimming industry.

The dieting industry responds to a need in that women who need to lose weight can find support and a structure in the form of clubs and magazines. However, the industry also exploits women's body dissatisfaction by treating their perceived problem as an actual problem and offering to solve it. It is also responsible for creating this problem in the first place. It is the perfect industry. By creating a market for itself it ensures that women will continue to feel fat and will continue to support the dieting industry.

Chapter 6

Do diets work?

The dieting world surrounds itself with a healthy glow of optimism. All diets are sold with the belief that 'you can do it' and 'this time you will lose weight'. It suggests that diets are a success and that losing weight is far more than just a vague possibility. Rosemary Conley's *Complete Hip and Thigh Diet* is full of success stories and readers' letters saying how much weight they have lost. Conley is totally confident, says 'I was determined to show that my diet *did* work' (p.28) and reports that the results from her questionnaire showed that 'none were disappointed' (p.37). Dr Lynch says of the principles outlined in his *BBC Diet* 'if you follow them, you *will* lose weight' (p.37). Weight loss is presented as a certainty. Yet evaluating how successful dieters actually are presents many problems.

HOW SUCCESSFUL ARE DIETERS?

A survey carried out in Britain suggests that about one in ten members of slimming clubs such as Weight Watchers and Slimming Magazine reach their target weight. However, it is difficult to understand what these figures actually mean. The clubs do not keep any information as to the weights of these women initially so there is no way of knowing how much weight they had to lose to be regarded as successes. In addition, the clubs cannot provide any information as to whether this includes all the women who drop out from lack of weight loss and whether it accounts for those who leave and then return for another try. It is possible that a woman who left and joined several times could be counted as many members.

One of the problems with assessing how successful dieters are at losing weight is evaluating how much these dieters wanted to lose in the first place. This raises the problem of whether they were obese, overweight or simply saw themselves as being fat. Most of the research into dieting successes has evaluated how much weight obese and overweight people lose. Assessing the effectiveness of dieting in average-weight women is difficult because such women tend either to diet on their own without medical or psychological help or their weight changes get lost amongst those of the obese.

In 1984 Dr Feinstein from Yale Medical School in America predicted that only about 12 per cent of patients who seek medical help for weight loss actually lose weight. He further predicted that about two out of this twelve maintained this weight loss. Comparing these figures with those for people who do not seek medical help also raises several problems. This number could be higher than in the average population which tries to lose weight, since it could be argued that patients who seek outside help are more determined to succeed and are faced with a life-threatening problem. Conversely, it could also be argued that they also have a greater weight problem which is more difficult to solve, suggesting that this number is lower than that for the success rate of the general public.

Perhaps it is necessary to evaluate dieting success in obese and average-weight people individually.

Weight loss in the obese and overweight

In 1958 Albert Stunkard predicted that '95 per cent of dieters regain weight five years after treatment'. In 1989 Dr Thomas Wadden and his colleagues in Philadelphia carried out a study to test this prediction. They reported the results of a five-year study in which they followed up a group of seventy-six obese women who had attempted to lose weight. A third of these women had been given a very low calorie diet for four months, a third had been given behaviour therapy involving a low calorie diet, rewards for when they lost weight and help to change their attitudes and behaviour towards food for six months, and a third had been given both, again for six months.

The initial weight loss for all the women was very similar, and they lost between 24 and 36 pounds over a six-month period. The women receiving both the very low calorie diet and behaviour therapy lost more weight than the women receiving either of these alone. However, after a year 95 per cent of the women receiving only the very low calorie diet and 64 per cent of the women receiving behaviour therapy had regained *some* of the lost weight. The group who received both forms of treatment showed a 68 per cent weight regain. After five years the majority of the women (64 per cent) had regained *all* the weight they had lost. In fact some of the subjects had actually gained weight, although three women did maintain all of their weight loss.

The results from this suggest that things are not quite as gloomy as predicted in 1958. However, even when women are involved in a strict regime with supervision and support, weight loss and in particular maintaining this weight loss is very difficult. Other studies have also investigated weight loss in the obese and have found similar results. In 1986 Dr Kramer and his colleagues found that 70 per cent of his obese dieters regained all the weight they had lost and a further study suggests that up to 81 per cent of obese dieters may weigh the same as they did before dieting.

This would suggest there is still no hard and fast set of rules for weight loss if you are obese. Dieting may result in initial weight loss but maintaining this loss is problematic. However, this does not mean that the obese and overweight should necessarily give up or stop asking for professional help. A lot of research is looking into more effective ways to help weight loss in those people who are threatening their health by being over-weight. The LEARN programme in America is a complex and comprehensive project for weight loss in the obese and over-weight. It emphasises life-style change and encourages an understanding of all aspects of weight and food, and focuses not only on eating but also on attitudes to food, mood and size. Although it is still relatively untested it certainly adds some optimism to a fairly disheartening area.

This difficulty in weight loss in the obese has implications for the many women who are attempting to lose weight, not because they are objectively overweight but because they perceive themselves as fat – the great majority of dieters. Dieting for the obese is in some ways easier than for the average-weight woman. Although obese women do have more weight to lose and need a longer period of concerted effort to reach their target weight, other factors contribute to making dieting that bit easier. For a start, severely overweight women will receive generalised social support; the important people in their lives will accept that they need to lose weight and will provide the support needed. They will not be surrounded by friends offering them food and telling them that they are fine as they are. They also have the additional motivation to lose weight derived from health worries and problems such as breathlessness and stiff joints. Most women are not motivated by these worries nor do they receive support and encouragement from everyone around them.

So how successful are dieters who are of average weight?

Weight loss in the average-weight dieter

Assessing how much weight is lost by average-weight dieters is very difficult. A lot of women diet on their own and do not receive outside help, resulting in a lack of records of their success or failure. It is also difficult to evaluate a successful diet in someone who does not objectively need to lose weight. If they lose half a stone is this success when no-one other than themselves thought they needed to lose it in the first place? Is it a greater success if they lose a stone? Probably the best way to evaluate success is to compare target weight with actual weight after dieting. This removes any subjective ideas about whether the dieter should be dieting and assesses the effectiveness of their intentions to lose weight.

Researchers have made various estimates as to how successful the average-weight dieter is at weight loss and maintaining this loss. Most of these evaluations seem to suggest that about 5 per cent of dieters lose and maintain any losses. However, any numbers are very difficult to interpret. Perhaps it is equally important to take account of individual case histories.

Below is a questionnaire aimed at assessing how successful the average-weight dieter is at losing weight. If you answer the questions the degree of success is self-evident. This is not an exercise in creating misery and disillusionment but is a useful way to evaluate behaviour.

Successful dieting

1 When did you first start dieting?
2 How many years ago was this?

3 How much did you weigh when you first started to diet?
4 How much did you want to weigh?
5 How much do you weigh now?
6 How much do you want to weigh now?

Examine the relationship between your answers. How does your present weight compare with how much you weighed when you first started to diet? How do your previous and present ideal weights compare? How many years of your life have you spent thinking about losing weight and trying to eat less? How successful has all this thinking been? Was it worth it?

If you feel that it has all been worth it, then congratulations! If you are not sure or feel that it certainly has not been worth all of the effort that you have put into it, then you are not alone.

SUCCESSFUL DIETING

The information on how many diets fail and how people of all shapes and sizes do not seem to lose weight is quite disheartening. Yet some people still seem to lose weight. Readers' success stories in magazines have to come from somewhere. Are these dieters in some way different? Are there factors which distinguish failed and successful dieters?

One factor which is a good predictor of weight loss is sex – not how much you have but whether you are male or female. Men have more success at both losing weight and maintaining any losses than women. As one spokeswoman from Slimmer Clubs said, 'Men tend to arrive at the clubs weighing more than most of the women there, they diet, lose weight and leave before most of the women who were there before them.' So why is this?

There are many factors which seem to predict weight loss and these are more likely to be characteristic of men than women.

So what are these factors?

The most obvious is the number of previous attempts at weight loss. Men seem to diet only once. They have not spent a lifetime trying to lose weight and this is a good predictor of weight loss. The fewer diets tried, the more likely you are to lose weight. If you diet, lose weight and then regain the weight, further weight loss becomes more difficult. This is because of changes in metabolic rate and the percentage of fat in the body and a process called weight cycling which is discussed in detail in

Chapter 7. Men diet once, have a high metabolic rate and a higher percentage of body muscle, and find it easier to lose weight.

Repeated dieting has other detrimental effects. Diets which result in no weight loss or regained lost weight create disillusionment. One of the best predictors of weight loss is believing that you can do it. Men who have never dieted before have not suffered the feelings of failure associated with constant dieting, and are therefore more likely to believe that dieting is easy and that they will succeed. This belief in their own success increases the likelihood that this success will occur.

The availability of food also predicts success or failure in dieting. Men are not usually surrounded by food, they do not have to cook and shop for the family, and are not constantly tempted to eat. When they decide to lose weight they can detach themselves from food and concentrate only on eating less. For women it is a different story. When women decide to diet they still have to cook and shop for the rest of the family and provide high calorie food for everyone else whilst they try to eat less.

Finally, men are not pressurised to be thin to the same degree as women. Men decide to diet at a much higher weight than their female counterparts. They therefore have an additional motivation to lose weight: health.

Of course, not all successful dieters are men and these factors which predict weight loss can also exist in women. Yet men are the embodiment of many of the factors which predict weight loss.

However, there are additional characteristics associated with success in dieting which are not necessarily characteristic of men.

An increase in exercise seems to predict success in weight loss. A recent study carried out in America showed that dieters who exercised were more likely to lose weight than dieters who just reduced their caloric intake. It was originally believed that exercise caused weight loss by using up calories. Exercise does burn up calories but only surprisingly few compared to an average meal. Professor Kelly Brownell has devised a chart to explain how many calories are used up in physical activity. He suggests that for a person who weighs 125 lbs, sleeping for ten minutes uses 10 calories, running at 5.5 miles per hour for ten minutes uses 90 calories and walking upstairs for ten minutes uses 146 calories. The average lunch probably takes about twenty minutes and probably consists of about 400 calories! Until recently it was also believed that exercise could raise your metabolic rate. However, recent evidence suggests that, although the metabolic rate may increase temporarily, this results only from prolonged and intensive exercise.

However, exercise still seems to predict weight loss, so why is this?

Exercise has many other effects which indirectly influence weight loss. Primarily, it helps to maintain muscle tissue whilst the body is losing fat. In addition, exercise can be fun and enjoyable and can provide a diversion from the problems of everyday life. Increased self-confidence contributes to a general feeling of self-control and can aid attempts at losing weight.

BUT FOR THE MAJORITY...

For most people dieting does not work. Whether they are obese, overweight or simply see themselves as being fat dieting does not help them to become thinner. Initial weight loss may occur but this is very often regained, making further weight loss more difficult.

The large majority of dieters are not obese nor are they overweight; they just see themselves as being overweight. And yet they persistently diet with the desire to be thinner. Their own experience of previous attempts at dieting tells them that they won't lose weight and yet we are constantly led to believe that 'this time it will be different'. But for the majority, this time it will be exactly the same.

For the obese and the overweight maybe there are additional reasons to persist, to try out the new programmes and to read the most recent literature, but for the majority of women, why continue doing something that does not work?

Chapter 7

Why do diets fail?

The dieting industry, doctors and folklore tell us that if you eat less then you will lose weight. We are told that it is a very simple equation involving energy into the body and energy used by the body. If the energy into the body is greater than the energy used, then you will gain weight, and if the energy used is greater than the energy going into the body then you will lose weight.

From our own observations we know that inhabitants of countries with food shortages eat less than those in the western world and are not overweight, and that anorexics successfully restrict their food intake and show massive weight loss. Yet when dieters try to eat less they very rarely lose weight. The *Daily Mail* said of a group of dieters 'the only reason they ended up fat and miserable was, I suspect, because they clearly didn't stick to their diet'. But is it as simple as this?

So why do so many diets fail?

As discussed in a previous chapter, most dieters seem to fluctuate between periods of eating less than non-dieters and periods of eating more.

It is difficult to assess exactly how much dieters do eat but first I want to consider why, if dieters do eat less than non-dieters and less than they would do if they were not dieting, the majority of them still do not lose weight.

THE METABOLIC EFFECTS OF EATING LESS

Dieting affects your metabolic rate. If you start to eat less your body slows down the rate at which it functions.

It is only relatively recently that there have been ample

amounts of food available to most people in the western world. In terms of human existence on earth we are still programmed to deal with droughts, food shortages and periods of starvation. It is far more damaging and more likely in evolutionary terms for the body to starve to death than it is to overeat. And so we have evolved with the perfect method for avoiding starvation during a period of food shortage: storing excess food when it is available. This excess food is stored mainly in the form of fat, which is oxidised to produce energy when needed.

Metabolic rate refers to the amount of energy made available for use for a specific period of time. Our metabolic rates are also perfectly adapted for food shortages. If we decrease our food intake our bodies prepare themselves for the anticipated assault on stored food. The metabolic rate decreases so that the body can function as efficiently as possible and therefore use as little energy as possible and as little stored fat. Dieting for a period of fourteen days can lead to a decline of up to 20 per cent of the metabolic rate.

A recent study at the Rockefeller University in New York examined the effects of dieting on dieters' daily energy requirements. A group of obese people were studied; they had lost substantial amounts of weight and yet were still overweight by an average of 86 pounds. They found that as they lost weight their daily energy requirements dropped accordingly. After they had lost an average of 124 pounds their calorie requirements had dropped by an average of 28 per cent to become lower than those of normal-weight people. As they lost weight their bodies were using any available food more efficiently.

Although irritating to the dieter who wishes to lose weight, it makes perfect sense to the body which is responding to an evolutionary history of dealing with the lack of food. Excess food is still only a relatively recent development, and the desire to be thin by rejecting food makes no sense to our sense of survival.

So, even if dieters are managing to eat less food than non-dieters and less than they would do if they were not dieting, dieting reduces their metabolic rate. Any food eaten is used more efficiently and the need for metabolising fat is minimalised. To lose weight and maintain this weight loss, dieters have to eat less consistently, and to compensate for a decreasing metabolic rate they have to eat less and less over time.

But what about the times when dieters are eating more than

non-dieters and perhaps even eating more than they would do if they were not dieting at all?

DIET-BREAKING

It is often assumed that diets do not work because the dieters are not actually dieting. The dieting industry tells us that failed dieters are weak-willed and are simply not sticking to their diet. The responsibility for not losing weight is placed firmly on the dieter's shoulders with no understanding of the processes which constitute diet-breaking.

Experimental work shows that dieters overeat both in the laboratory and in naturalistic studies. Perhaps this behaviour is an illustration of diet-breaking, suggesting that not sticking to a diet is a far more complex issue than simply a lack of determination.

So why do dieters not stick to their diets? Surely all they have to do is eat less food?

Anyone who has ever dieted can provide you with reams of reasons why they break their diets, and will cite hundreds of examples of times when they have eaten more than they intended. Dieters may recall the different causes for their episodes of 'over-indulgence' and yet most dieters still blame themselves, and regard themselves as failures.

For the rest of this chapter I want to draw upon the results of an experiment that I carried out as part of my work for my PhD, which suggests that diet-breaking is not the fault of the dieter, it does not reflect personal inadequacy, but is an inevitable consequence of the structure of dieting. Overeating is part and parcel of attempting to diet and is a consequence of trying to eat less, a direct product of dieting.

I carried out a study in the final year of my PhD which examined the effects of dieting and attempted to find out why so many diets fail and why women break their diets. The overeating behaviour shown by dieters in the laboratory is also reported by dieters in their day-to-day lives. Many women report fluctuating between days when they manage to eat less and days when they completely overeat.

Imagine sticking to 1000 calories a day for three days and then being invited out to dinner on the fourth day. Tempted by all the food available and the fact it is a special occasion, many dieters say that they would eat more at the dinner than if they hadn't been trying to diet on the previous days. It is like thinking 'Oh what the hell. If I'm going to break my diet I might as well make the most of it.' It is similar to trying to give up smoking or drinking.

A friend of mine used to smoke only after six in the evening. She would never think about a cigarette before this and certainly wouldn't think of smoking first thing in the morning. At New Year she decided to stop smoking. From the moment she decided to stop all she could think about was cigarettes, even in the morning. She woke up desperate to smoke and found that when she actually had one cigarette, for the first few days of smoking again, she smoked more than ever before. The overeating found in dieters is similar to this.

It was originally believed that overeating was followed by a period of dieting, that people dieted because they had a tendency to overeat, and needed to compensate for episodes of indulgence. As discussed in Chapter 2, dieters are all sorts of people. Some have problems with food, but the vast majority of dieters simply see themselves as being larger than society tells them to be. There is no evidence to suggest that dieters become dieters because they have episodes of overeating.

It was then proposed that dieting caused overeating – a complete reversal of the original theory. Researchers suggested that the overeating shown by dieters in the laboratory and reported in their day-to-day lives was a direct consequence of attempting to eat less. This is similar to the analogy with smoking; trying to stop smoking causes a desire to smoke more and trying to stop eating causes overeating. The difference is that stopping smoking is good for you, stopping eating isn't!

This idea was called the causal analysis of eating behaviour and suggests that attempting not to eat, paradoxically, increases the probability of overeating, the specific behaviour dieters are attempting to avoid. It represented a new approach to the eating behaviour of dieters and is an interesting reappraisal of the situation.

A study by Wardle and Beales in 1988 showed that dieters tended to overeat and the authors concluded that the results 'supported the idea that dieting causes disturbances of food intake'.

So why does this happen? Why does dieting cause overeating?

It is possible that overeating is a direct product of changes which occur as a result of dieting. Dieting could cause changes which increase the tendency to eat more.

It has been predicted from the causal analysis of dieting and overeating that increasing dieting would cause an increase in those factors related to overeating. Research suggests that changes in mood, state of mind, control and hunger occur as a consequence of dieting and could cause an increase in eating.

A classic study was carried out in 1950 by an American professor called Ancel Keys and his colleagues. Their aim was to evaluate the effects of a period of restricting calories, and to see whether reducing food intake caused overeating. Over a period of twelve weeks, thirty-six healthy non-dieting men received a carefully controlled daily food intake of approximately half their normal intake and consequently lost 25 per cent of their original body weight. Ancel Keys states that they developed a pre-occupation with food, often resulting in their hoarding or stealing it. They showed an inability to concentrate, with mood changes such as depression and apathy being common. At the end of the period of dieting the men were allowed to eat freely and often ate continuously. They reported loss of control over their eating behaviour, sometimes resulting in binge eating. The author concluded that these psychological effects were not a function of the actual process of starvation, but were more likely to be due to the restriction of their diet.

In 1988, Warren and Cooper, in a study in Cambridge assessing the effects of dieting on both mood and the control of eating, placed seven men and seven women on a calorie-restricted diet for two weeks, and monitored any daily changes. They found an increase in feelings of loss of control, over eating and increased preoccupation with food.

Dieting seems to cause overeating by changing factors which contribute to eating more. The study which I carried out attempted to assess what these factors could be.

Up to 90 per cent of the female population diet at some time in their lives. The aim of the study was to examine the effects of these constant attempts at losing weight and to analyse their contribution to overeating. The failure to lose weight is often regarded as a sign of weakness and an indication that the dieter is not dieting properly. The following results suggest that failed dieters are simply responding to changes which occur during a diet and that breaking your diet is inevitable.

The method of the study

Twenty-three women were recruited for the study from the nurses, secretaries and administrative staff at the Institute of Psychiatry in London. I advertised for volunteers who were intending to try and lose weight for summer, and had no problems finding enough women! The hospital dietitian gave all the women an interesting and informative talk on what constitutes a healthy and nutritional diet and advised them to stick to between 1000 and 1500 calories a day. All the women devised their own diet to fit in with their life-styles which meant that the study was as naturalistic as possible. The diets chosen very much reflected how the women would have chosen to lose weight even if the study had not taken place.

At the beginning of the dieting period of six weeks, all the women felt very enthusiastic and positive. They felt that 'this time they were going to succeed' and 'this time it would be different'. There was a strong feeling of mutual support, and a recognition that everyone was in the same boat and could understand how the others were feeling. Rating scales recorded changes in mood, state of mind, hunger and preoccupation with food and weight, and an interview involved general questions about the diet and more specific questions relating to how the diet was going and whether they had broken it at all.

So what does happen when you diet? Do you start to overeat and what changes accompany this overeating?

Preoccupation with food

When discussing the effects of the study carried out in America, Keys and his colleagues said: 'Food in all its ramifications became the principal topic of conversation, reading, and daydreams for almost all. . . subjects.'

The first change that became obvious for the women in my study was that they became preoccupied with food.

As women, in a society where we are expected to shop, cook and provide food for our families, food already plays a central role in our lives. It becomes a way to show love and affection to our dependants and a way to ask for love from those we are dependent on. If we provide dinner for our husbands when they come home from work (even if we ourselves have been working!) it shows that we appreciate that they have been working hard (and, it suggests, even harder than us) and that we recognise how much they do for us. Children learn from a very early age that eating their mother's food makes her feel positive and valued. They also learn that to refuse her food is rejecting her love and will make her anxious and upset. We think about food in terms way beyond the limitations of feeling hungry and needing sustenance.

And yet when dieting, this food has to be avoided. The aim of dieting is to eat less of the substance which plays a central role in our family and social lives. Endless lists of foods become forbidden. Cream cakes, chocolate, chips, pastry, dairy products and take-aways are all outside the limitations set by the diet. They become special and treats. They are even advertised as treats; remember the 'naughty but nice' adverts! And the obvious result of anything being 'forbidden' is that it becomes far more attractive than it ever was before. And therefore we want to eat it more than we ever did before. Dieters do not crave salads; they crave high calorie foods – the very food they are trying to avoid. Their attention is focused on the stuff they cannot have.

And to make things worse, not only are they not supposed to eat high calorie foods, most dieters still have to provide them for everyone else. If dieters could live in a world where everyone ate 1000 calories a day, where families did not feel rejected and annoyed if mum stopped buying biscuits and where high calorie foods were not presented as being exciting, then dieters might have an easier time of it.

However, they don't. Not only are we a society which is already obsessed with food, but trying not to eat it makes it more attractive, and makes us more preoccupied than ever before.

Many of the women who took part in the study said that having to cook for others made sticking to the diet very difficult.

One woman gave a dinner party for several friends and felt that she had eaten more than her diet allowed. She said: 'I did not want to give in, but I felt that after preparing a three-course meal for everyone else, the least I could do was enjoy my efforts.'

Another women said: 'It's Sunday and I'm cooking for the kids so I might as well have some, rather than make something else for myself.' She felt that since she had already made the effort in cooking one meal, why should she bother to cook another?

Food plays a central role in family life. Trying not to eat it when you still have to cook for everyone makes dieting very difficult.

Several other women said that they needed to cook and eat with their family to show how much they cared.

One woman said that she treated her daughter to a hamburger lunch and that 'I didn't want to feel isolated, and it was nice just having lunch together'.

Another felt that she had 'to feed the family properly' and that 'it is a sign of love if my husband gets a nice meal'.

For women, love and the family are already intrinsically tied up with food. Trying to diet means attempting to stop seeing food in the usual way, and trying not to think about something which is central to our lives. Dieting makes us more preoccupied with something which is already central to our lives as women.

And the consequence of being preoccupied with food?

Food becomes the focus for rewards, for treats and for comfort. The more we try to diet the more we think about food. And the more we think about it, maybe. . .the more we eat. Diet-breaking becomes understandable.

Preoccupation with weight

The second obvious change which happens to dieters is that they become preoccupied and obsessed with their weight. The original motivation to lose weight is complex and yet the main focus is to feel and look more attractive and to feel in control.

Yet dieting shifts the focus from feeling and looking better to what the scales say. Weight/height charts do not say that your ideal weight is when you feel good about yourself. They say you should weigh 8 stone 3½ pounds or 9 stone 2 pounds. They precisely select and advise a weight for you. Every women has a different bone structure, a different facial structure and is a different age. What may suit a 30-year-old would make a 45-year-old look scrawny, and yet the dieting industry sells us a specific weight as if we are all the same.

Dieters become slaves to the scales. Dieters often feel very positive after a week of sticking to their diet. They feel good about themselves and feel in control. I met one such woman who came to be interviewed feeling happy and successful and proud of her week's attempt at dieting. She got on the scales enthusiastically and the pleasure drained out of her as they read the same as they had done the week before. She felt defeated and useless just because her weight hadn't changed. The fact that a few moments before she had felt fine was forgotten and her mood was totally controlled by the number pointed to by the needle. Her weight had become the most important thing, not just feeling good and in control.

Judy Mazel, in *The Beverly Hills Diet*, perfectly describes this obsession with the scales. She says that the scales have 'more effect on us than an atom bomb' and describes how the number on the scales can alter the dieter's reality:

> When I looked in the mirror my hip bones had vanished. . .I was terrified. The whale that I had once been was looming. I inched onto the scale with dread and horror. With one eye shut, barely breathing, I looked down. Three numbers stared up at me – 102. I had not gained an ounce! . . . I was overcome with joy and relief, and when I looked in the mirror again, my hip bones had reappeared.

Judy Mazel's reality was determined, not by how she felt about herself, but by how the scales said that she should feel about herself.

Weight watching and slimming clubs rely on and create this obsession with weight. The motivations for dieting are complex but the focus is on weight loss. Dieters are lined up and weighed in front of strangers and congratulated if their weight has gone down. They are not congratulated if they are feeling good about themselves, even though this was a major original motivating factor for their attempts at dieting.

So what happens if you become preoccupied with weight?

First of all it leads to forgetting why you wanted to diet. Life becomes ruled by the scales and improving your self-esteem takes second place. Perhaps more importantly, preoccupation with weight contributes to the general process of diet-breaking.

Weight fluctuations occur for a multitude of reasons. In the first week of dieting many dieters can lose up to 7 pounds. This often acts as a great motivator to continue dieting and raises the dieter's expectations of future weight loss. However, more than half of this is water, about a quarter muscle and only a quarter fat, the stuff dieters are trying to get rid of. Once the excess water has gone from the body the following week's weight loss will be much less, if any. If the dieter is preoccupied with her weight, this will come as a shock, and she will be disheartened.

Dieters rely on the scales for reinforcement and recognition of their efforts and yet weight changes often seem erratic and unfair. Feeling disillusioned with the diet, dieters 'go out for dinner because I can't be bothered making all that effort for nothing any more' and break their diet, a perfectly understandable response to their unrewarded suffering.

A main cause of weight fluctuation is pre-menstrual water retention. Many women retain water just before their periods. This is usually experienced as feeling bloated and finding that your clothes feel a bit tighter than usual. If you are dieting it is also experienced as a 2-pound weight gain, just enough to make you fed-up with your dieting efforts. It is surprising that, even though women are perfectly aware that the excess weight is water retention and will go in a few days, dieters still feel that they are to blame, see it as a failure.

Feeling a failure can lead to overeating.

Reaction to foods

Dieters become preoccupied with the very substance they are trying to avoid – food. Not all foods, but those which are forbidden and outside the limitations set by the diet. Dieters see these foods as more exciting and pleasurable, and they become increasingly so if they are not eaten for a while.

A well-documented behaviour shown by dieters suggests that if they do actually eat a forbidden food, such as a chocolate bar or a piece of cake, they will then eat more food after it than if they had not eaten that piece of chocolate in the first place. You would expect them to eat less.

Many studies have been carried out both in America and Britain to illustrate this paradoxical behaviour, during which dieters are asked to consume a high calorie food. This is often very hard for the experimenter to do, although not as unethical as it may seem since the dieters always have the choice to say no. They are then asked to take part in a 'taste test' and to sample a selection of foods. The dieters are left alone in a room so they can eat as little or as much as they like. The amount they eat is then measured. It has been found that if the dieters are given a 'forbidden food' before the taste test, they eat more during the taste test than if they had been given a neutral food such as a cream cracker. This is paradoxical – you would imagine that they would feel fuller and therefore eat less. The non-dieters *do* eat less.

Dieting causes dieters to respond differently to forbidden foods; forbidden foods trigger overeating. Imagine dieting for two weeks, sticking to a diet of low calorie foods, eating less than people around you and missing out on social eating and family dinners. A friend has a party, and before you is a wonderful display of all the foods you have been avoiding. I am not going to eat, you tell yourself. Just one sausage roll, you tell yourself, just one plate of trifle. And before you know it you have eaten two whole platesful, way beyond your limits set for the evening. Is this because you are simply weak-willed? Is it simply because you cannot control yourself? If you hadn't been dieting in the first place all that food wouldn't have appeared so exciting. One plateful would have been enough; you would have felt full and too involved in enjoying the evening to concentrate on eating.

Yet dieting changes this. The foods which dieting have made forbidden cause you to eat more than if you had not been dieting at all. They trigger a reaction. And this reaction is overeating.

So what has dieting changed?

Dieting changes the thoughts that go through your head when you eat the first 'forbidden food'. Instead of just enjoying eating it, dieters find that certain foods trigger specific thoughts. I asked several women what they thought after eating something that they felt they shouldn't have.

'Now I've eaten that I might as well make the most of it' was common. Dieters see the episode of overeating as an isolated event which they cram full of food.

'I'm sick of having to diet, I'm just going to eat loads.' A lot of women said that they felt like rebelling against the diet. They felt angry at having to worry about food and their weight and wanted to have a good time. They ate to rebel against the pressures which tell them they shouldn't eat, and to show that at that time they were no longer going to conform.

'Now I've eaten that I might as well give in to all the drives to eat.' Many women felt that, whilst they are dieting, all the drives to eat well up inside and a constant effort is required to ignore them. They felt that it was a balance between the drive to eat and the drive to diet, and that eating a forbidden food meant that the drive to eat won. It broke down their resistance and they ate enough to compensate – and more – for all the times when they had eaten less than they wanted to.

One woman said 'I'm fed up with saying no all the time. I want to eat normally. Why should I deprive myself of nice food?' She felt that she wanted to react against all the pressure to be thin by asserting herself and eating like everyone else. She said 'Everything is focused on food, your body and other people's perception of your body. Eating is saying "to hell with all that pressure". Why is my acceptance conditional on me having a nice body?'

Dieting makes high calorie foods become treats, and these treats seem to trigger a chain of thoughts which can lead to overeating. In a study by Dr King and her colleagues in 1987 dieters and non-dieters were asked to rate different types of food for a variety of qualities. They found that the dieters were more likely to see foods in terms of guilt than the non-dieters.

In addition, these foods seem directly to change the way dieters feel about themselves. In a study carried out in 1989 the researchers examined the effects of eating on body image. They found that not only did the dieters show a more negative body image but that this body image became more negative after eating a high calorie meal. It would seem that not only do dieters respond to specific foods by overeating but these foods also directly affect their body image.

These reactions to food would never happen if the dieters were not trying to eat less in the first place. They would eat what they wanted when they wanted and food would not take on such an important role in their lives. Dieting means that food becomes attractive and yet it has to be avoided. It is like an elastic band. Hold it back, then let it go and all the energy needed to retain it is released. If it is not held back in the first place there is no energy to be released. Food becomes a trigger to the behaviour dieters want to avoid – eating – and eating becomes the trigger to further eating.

Emotions

Dieting changes your mood and mood changes can cause overeating. Dieters often report feeling positive and motivated at the beginning of a diet. It provides a structure and a goal, and a way to confront life's problems. However, dieting can also cause misery and feelings of inadequacy.

Women set themselves targets. They aim for a specific rate of weight loss and decide that all they have to do is eat less! However, it is not as simple as this and not losing weight or diet-breaking is depressing. Not being able to achieve these goals can make you feel a failure. Diet-breaking is understood in terms of being weak-willed, and this idea is promoted by the dieting industry which suggests that weight loss is a sign of control, thinness is a sign of control, and not sticking to its diet sheets is due to weakness and not the fault of its diet.

Dieting also disrupts family and social life. So many of life's pleasurable activities are centred on eating. A celebration involves dinner, and a family get-together revolves around the dinner table. Yet dieting means denying yourself these pleasures. Having to watch others whilst you tuck into your defrosted, pre-packed, microwaved, low calorie meal is not much fun. Shopping for others and buying yourself a special lettuce is frustrating, and lettuce after carrot is boring.

Dieting is depressing. You miss out on so much and, while constant self-denial may be rewarding in a nunnery, for the majority it results in feeling fed-up, bored and isolated.

Many women said that the whole experience of dieting and diet-breaking was quite upsetting.

One woman said: 'I'm just totally hopeless and weak, and though I hate being fat, I just don't have the willpower to do anything about it.' She hated herself for not losing weight, and felt inadequate and depressed because she could not stick to her diet.

Other women called themselves 'a dustbin and a pig', 'disgusting' and 'depressed that something as simple as eating cannot be controlled'.

One woman said: 'I feel weak and ashamed that I let myself down.' She felt disappointed with herself and inadequate.

Several women also said that they found dieting depressing because they didn't get any support from anyone else, in particular their husbands or boyfriends.

Many women diet because they want to be more attractive and they believe that if they lose weight their partners will appreciate the difference. In fact, many women are told to diet by the men in their lives. Recently on a popular television programme I was angered to see an attractive middle-aged slim woman being told to lose weight by her overweight husband. She told the chat show host that what she wanted most in the world was the perfect body, because it would make her husband happy. 'He thinks my thighs are too big', she said. He sat there nodding away in agreement, oblivious to his own fat thighs.

However, many women find that when they try to lose weight their husbands are not at all supportive.

One woman said: 'I'm annoyed that my husband doesn't encourage me. I wanted to prove to him that I could do it.' Her husband felt that she should lose weight and yet did not make the process of weight loss any easier. He resented the fact that she bought low calorie food and felt deprived because the cupboards were not as well stocked as usual. He also said that she had tried to diet so many times before and not lost weight and why should this time be any different? On the one hand, husbands can make women feel overweight either by casual comments or by directly suggesting that they diet, and yet when it comes to dieting they find the whole process irritating.

Another woman said that her boyfriend actually encouraged her to break her diet. He used to make endless comments about her size and then when she started to lose weight he would buy her food and offer to take her out for dinner. In fact, he seemed quite worried that she might actually become thinner. He appeared to be threatened by other men and was worried that if she lost weight she would leave him for someone else. He thought that she was fat, but was frightened of her becoming thinner.

This feeling that they did not get any support from husbands and boyfriends was quite a common complaint, and seemed to add to the difficulty of dieting and feelings of inadequacy from not losing weight.

And the consequence of these mood changes? – eating. Feeling fed-up can reduce your determination to eat less. The drives to eat outweigh the drives to restrain and diet-breaking occurs. Depression lowers your resistance and the pleasures of eating become greater.

It was originally believed that fat people ate differently from thin people and in particular ate for comfort. It was believed that food reduced their depression and provided a source of security and a reward. It now seems that regardless of weight most people eat for comfort and find food a reward. In particular, this is true of dieters. Dieters' self-denial is rewarded with food, weight loss is rewarded with food, and feeling fed-up is compensated for with food. Dieters alleviate the depression caused by dieting with eating. They eat more to eradicate the low mood caused by trying to eat less. Dieting becomes its own worst enemy. It causes changes in mood which themselves cause diet-breaking and overeating.

Dieting causes misery. It causes feelings of failure, inadequacy and isolation. Eating helps to reduce these feelings.

Effects of dieting on eating control

Dieting causes problems with the control of food intake. Attempting to diet results in increased calorie consumption in certain situations. Dieters feel more out of control than non-dieters, and experience chaotic eating patterns.

Dieters aim to eat less and to control their food intake. Women often attribute their perceived 'large size' to their inability to eat appropriately, believing that the reason why they are over their desired weight is because they overeat. Women look at other people's eating behaviour and believe that they eat less and at different times and understand their own behaviour in terms of loss of control. Dieting is regarded as a means to impose self-control and an external structure on their food intake. However, there is no evidence to suggest that, before dieting, women who are over their desired weight eat any differently or experience more episodes of loss of control than women who are at their desired weight. There is no evidence to suggest that larger women are more out of control than their thinner counterparts, or that women who decide to diet have experienced more over-eating than those who don't.

However, there is evidence to suggest that dieting increases episodes of both perceived and actual loss of control. Imposing the dieting structure on food intake appears to have the opposite to the desired effect.

Perceived loss of control

Because of the limitations set by the diet, any food which is eaten beyond these limits is regarded as overeating and attributed to loss of control. Eating which would usually be seen as a large meal, a special occasion or a treat is regarded as overeating and indicative of lost control. The urge to eat which would usually be regarded as hunger is registered in terms of craving, and giving in to this urge is regarded as a weakness.

One woman said: 'When I start to diet I want to eat things I shouldn't eat. I want to buy fattening foods when I know I am on a diet.' She did not eat any more than before she began to diet; however, desires to eat certain foods are perceived as being a problem.

Actual loss of control

One of the main effects of dieting is that it contributes to actual loss of control over eating. Dieting causes increases in the pre-occupation with food, making food more attractive, it alters responses to food, resulting in certain foods becoming 'forbidden', which triggers specific states of mind, and it causes mood changes. All these contribute to actual loss of control and result in the dieter eating more than she would have if she hadn't dieted in the first place.

One woman said that she found the diet very difficult. 'I feel depressed about dieting. I overate to start off with, felt depressed and then ate more. I felt that eating would make me happier, but I just felt guilty and wanted more to eat.' Dieting resulted in her eating more than if she had not tried to diet in the first place.

Another woman said: 'I can't cope at the moment with the feelings of deprivation that I get when I go on a diet. It wells up inside me and I panic and eat.' The diet made her feel deprived, and so even though she wasn't eating less, she then ate more to compensate.

Dieting aims to control food intake and to reduce food consumption. It aims to impose a structure on the dieter's behaviour and to result in weight loss. It doesn't appear to achieve either of these aims. The cognitive and emotional changes which occur as a response to dieting undermine attempts at eating less, and cause overeating, the very behaviour dieters are trying to avoid.

DIETING – THE VICIOUS CIRCLE

So what are the consequences of all this failed dieting? How do dieters respond to diet-breaking?

Dieting becomes a vicious circle, a merry-go-round which is difficult to get off. And each time around the effects are more powerful, more destructive and the weight loss less.

Effects of long-term dieting

If dieters are not really losing weight, what are they actually doing? It seems that all dieters have one thing in common: they are thinking about dieting. They are thinking about eating less and thinking about losing weight, but not necessarily achieving either of these aims. Sometimes dieters lose weight and sometimes they don't, but they are constantly trying to. Dieters share a common state of mind.

In the short term, dieting can provide a structure, a means of encouragement and support and a way to change your life. In the long term, failed dieting results in depression, a preoccupation with weight and food and episodes of overeating.

A recently documented effect of dieting is a process called weight cycling. This applies to those women who sometimes manage to lose weight but find that they put it back on again.

Have you ever dieted, lost weight and put back on more weight?

Have you ever dieted, lost weight, put it back on and next time around found it more difficult to lose?

Researchers at the University of Pennsylvania are involved in a weight cycling project to test the effects of 'yo-yo' dieting. Because so many dieters have reported that losing weight becomes progressively more difficult after putting weight back on, they first studied this effect in rats.

Researchers overfed a group of twenty-one rats to make them put on weight. They then changed their diet to make them lose this weight. They repeated this several times so that the rats went through a series of weight loss and weight regain. The first time around the rats took twenty-one days of dieting to reach their normal weight and forty-five days to regain the lost weight. The second time around the rats took forty-six days to lose the same amount of weight, eating the same amount of food, and only fourteen days to regain the weight. Prolonged dieting meant that weight became easier to regain and more difficult to lose.

A similar study was carried out at Harvard Medical School and it was found that the pattern was similar for dieting women. It seems that repeated weight loss causes the body to use up stored fat more efficiently, and to live off less food. Repeated dieting and weight regain put the body into 'starvation mode', the metabolic rate decreases, and even when the weight has been regained the body still expects further deprivation.

Further research suggests that 'yo-yo dieting' has even more disturbing consequences. Yo-yo dieters seem to lose their pounds as muscle and regain them as fat. Thus prolonged attempts at dieting increase the body's overall fat content. A study of 1170 men in Pennsylvania found that over a period of twenty-five years those who showed the greatest weight fluctuations had the highest risk of heart disease.

In the short term dieting may make you feel good. In the long term it can result in far more problems than it solves. If you don't lose any weight you will feel a failure, dieting will become a habit and a way of life, and you will experience all the psychological changes which seem to accompany attempts at losing weight. If you do manage to lose weight, unless you can keep it off for ever, further weight loss will be more difficult and the physical and psychological problems greater than the simple problem of seeing yourself as fatter than you would like to be.

Dieting causes overeating. Overeating causes weight gain. Weight gain causes dieting. In fact, dieting no longer seems to refer to eating less. What most people are doing when they 'diet' is a combination of eating less and eating more. They swing from times of restricting food to times of compensating for this restriction. Dieting means attempting to eat less, but not necessarily doing so. What all dieters have in common is a state of mind. They are thinking about eating less – that is all. Very few dieters actually manage to do this; most of them simply think about it. And this is why the dieting industry is so powerful. Dieters never finish dieting. Dieters never get to the stage when they can finish with the dieting industry. Because dieting means further dieting and therefore further use of the ever growing industry which supports it.

Chapter 8

Men and dieting

A couple of years ago I was explaining my area of research at a job interview. After I had given what I considered a clear and full account of my work, the only man in the room said 'There is an obvious logical error in your work'. I was totally taken aback and meekly asked what it was. 'What about men?' he said. I had never really considered men in relation to dieting before. My interest in the area stems from being a woman myself, and I always felt that it was nice to work on something that men hadn't managed to monopolise yet. This chapter is a concession to that male interviewer, and to the many other men who have told me 'it's just as bad for men'.

Men also have role models and heroes. Over the centuries, literature has been full of ever changing images of the ideal man. In 1813 Jane Austen wrote in *Pride and Prejudice*:

> Mr Darcy soon drew the attention of the room by his fine, tall person, handsome features, noble mien; and the report which was in general circulation within five minutes after his entrance, of his having ten thousand a year.

Attractive men were tall, straight and rich.

In the 1950s Charles Atlas used to be the ideal man. Men were sold work-out kits and body-building equipment. They had to be large, powerful and strong. They were men of few words and lots of muscles. But what is the message now? Do men have an image that they have to conform to?

It is often assumed that the media focus only on women's bodies in their attempts to sell a wide variety of products. Most adverts still have women modelling anything from clothes to cars to cleaning fluid. I asked several men if they felt there were pressures on men to look a certain way.

One 25-year-old NHS manager immediately replied: 'Definitely' and proceeded to provide a detailed description of the ideal man:

You have to be tall, in a sharp suit (casual but smart), exuding money. The ideal body is well built, wide shoulders, a v-shaped back tapering to a firm bottom with dimples and a flat stomach.

He felt that men used to be proud of their beer guts but now they were ashamed and hid them.

Another 25-year-old man said that the ideal man was summed up by the actor Richard Gere: 'Not over-muscular, fit and at fighting weight. So that you don't really notice his body, but it is capable of doing what it's supposed to do without impairing itself.' He felt that the ideal body was to do with fitness and health. He felt that the ideal body was one that was not noticeable because it was 'how a man's body should be'. Another felt that the ideal man was 'lithe, fit, stubbly and dark haired'.

I also asked several men what these images meant to them. The most common answer was that being tall, thin and fit meant that you were in control, and control was central to the 1990s' image of the ideal man. It also meant that you were healthy and confident and therefore capable of being a success in all other areas of life.

With the rise of the 1980s' work ethic, men in the media have become leaner; they look hard working and healthy. The ideal man does not self-indulge, he is in control and in command of his life. Hedonism seems to be becoming a thing of the past and this is illustrated by the contemporary ideal man.

So where do these images come from? These pressures seem to come from three sources: other men, women and the media.

One man said: 'Other men joke about putting on weight. They say "you're letting yourself go a bit" or suggest that you should take up squash at lunchtime.'

Another said, 'You overhear women talking about firm bottoms and flat stomachs and you realise that that's what they expect.' He also said: 'You know that women find certain film stars attractive. You also realise that they know nothing about them apart from how they look and what their bodies are like, so you realise that it is their bodies that make them attractive.'

The pressure also comes from the media. Over recent years there has been an increase in men used in advertising, all of whom are thin and stereotypically attractive. Media men have become less hedonistic and increasingly in control and reserved. In a recent television advert, a young man is used to advertise healthy pre-cooked meals. He is thin, healthy and represents clean living and self-control. He looks sensible. Male heroes of the 1960s and 1970s had an air of excess and debauchery about them. Now men are tame and controlled. The only media man that any of the men I interviewed could think of who was outside this image was Jack Nicholson who personifies total hedonism, self- indulgence and pleasure. Perhaps his attractiveness comes from his obvious rejection of social norms, and his ability not to conform, not to use tricks and not to be influenced by what other people expect.

Women tend to assume that men can get away with a greater variety of looks, sizes and shapes than women. It is believed that the male personality can compensate for many (but not all) physical characteristics. Woody Allen is a sex symbol; the female equivalent would never have even made it through the studio door. However, the media do seem to present an image of the ideal man of the 1980s and 1990s. How do men respond to these images? Do men feel dissatisfied with their bodies?

In 1968 Diabiase and Hjelle carried out a study to evaluate men's idea of the ideal body size. Groups of fat, average and thin men were shown silhouettes of male bodies which were also fat, thin and of average weight. The men were then asked to say which size they preferred and why. All the male subjects regardless of their own size preferred the average weight. They felt that both the thin and fat bodies represented qualities such as being shy, dependent and withdrawn, whereas the average-size body represented being active, energetic and dominant.

The men in the study showed a preference for a particular size. But was this reflected in a dissatisfaction with their own size?

In a study in 1988, described in Chapter 3, men and women were asked to rate their ideal size and their actual size. All the women subjects showed a large discrepancy between how they felt they looked and how they wanted to look, but the young men in the study did not. Regardless of their actual size, they felt satisfied with their weight.

Although men may report an ideal size and a preference for a particular body size this does not seem to be reflected in a dissatisfaction with their own size. It would seem that men are not directly affected with worries about their weight. I interviewed one man who was 30, six foot three, weighed 15 stone and would prefer to weigh 13 stone. Although he said he would prefer to weigh less, he felt that his weight was not that important. He said: 'I don't feel that my fatness has any effect on my attractiveness. Size and attractiveness are separate. People don't notice.'

I also asked him if being heavier than he wanted to be affected how he felt about himself. He replied: 'My self-esteem comes from being able to function to a standard set by myself both in my job and socially. Attractiveness comes from attitudes and personality.' He did admit that he felt more attractive in nice clothes but that 'people are more interested in what you have between your ears than in muscle'.

I interviewed another man who was five foot eleven and weighed 13½ stone. He said: 'Although I would like to be lighter I don't get depressed about it. I'm more concerned about being fit since there are so many other qualities related to my attractiveness. If I lost a stone I wouldn't be or feel any more attractive, I would simply be a stone lighter.'

He also felt that his worries about his weight were 'my own silly concerns, no one else notices or is affected by how much I weigh. My attractiveness is associated with many other factors.'

Although these men would have preferred to weigh less this did not influence how attractive they felt.

I also interviewed a 26-year-old man who was 10½ stone and five foot eleven. He wanted to be a stone heavier. I asked him if he felt that this affected his feelings of attractiveness. He felt that, even though he was aware of the ideal man: 'I am not strongly influenced by how men are supposed to look. The world of looking good is a completely separate world to mine and I choose to have no contact with it. I don't really think about attractiveness any more, there are too many other things to worry about.'

Self-satisfaction can be understood in terms of body image and self-image and the relationship between the two. Body image simply refers to the individual's satisfaction with their body, whereas self-image is a more global concept relating to a form of general self-appreciation. Perhaps self-satisfaction reveals a difference between men and women. Women's weight has a greater effect on their body image which in turn has a greater influence on their self-image. Although men may prefer to be of a certain weight, this has little effect on their body image, which is therefore not detrimental to their self-image.

However, some men do report a concern about their weight. I interviewed a 25-year-old man who was six foot three and weighed 15 stone. His ideal weight was about 12½ stone. I asked him why he wanted to be thinner.

I would feel better about myself. It's not to do with health, but mainly to be attractive to women. Fat is unattractive. When I take my clothes off in front of someone I don't feel embarrassed but neither do I feel proud. I think 'I hope they don't mind and still want to go through with this'.

He felt that being his size was not 'a good selling point'.

So how do men respond to their dissatisfaction with their weight? Two per cent of Weight Watchers' members are men. So men do not seem to go to clubs. But do they diet at home?

I interviewed one man who said:

I don't really do anything, I just worry about it. I try to eat less and drink wine instead of beer, but it's more a matter of thinking about it than doing anything....I would like to be thinner, but I don't want to pay the price. It is not worth the sacrifices.

Another man who was two stone heavier than his preferred weight said: 'I sometimes think about eating less but I never really manage it. It is too much effort.' Yet another who was a stone heavier than he wanted to be said: 'I undereat continuously. I can't remember the last time I ate till I was full. I find it difficult giving up things I really enjoy such as butter, but I generally cut down and eat salad.' However, he did add that he ate salad in addition to other foods!

What else do they do? Most men seem to get fit or go jogging rather than actually diet. They try to change their bodies through exercise not eating less. Maybe this is because food does not play such a central role in their lives, maybe it is more acceptable for women to say 'I'm on a diet'. But they are still pressurised to conform to a specific shape.

If weight is a concern for some men, maybe they also worry about other physical characteristics.

In 1955 a study was carried out to see which parts of the body were of most importance to men and women. Whilst women focused on hips, thighs and waist, the results for the men showed that their equivalent weak point was their height. Height seemed to be the factor which had the greatest effect on their body image. Men associated height with power, sexual strength and intellectual capacity.

Society expects a man to be taller than his female partner, and associates male height with other desirable qualities such as authority and social status. A study in 1968 evaluated the relationship between perceived height and power. Students were introduced to a Mr England and were told that he was either a fellow student, a lecturer, a senior lecturer or a professor. They were then asked to estimate his height. The results showed that his estimated height increased with his supposed seniority. Height was associated with power. Interestingly, this association also extends to politics. As a sociologist, Feldman, said in 1971, 'It is not by chance that every American president since 1900 has been the taller of the two major political candidates.' In addition, in 1960, American voters were asked whom they preferred, and whom they thought was the taller out of Kennedy and Nixon. It was found that preference and perceived height went together.

Why is height so important?

On the whole, men are up to 5 – 10 per cent taller than women. Girls tend to have finished their significant growth by the time they reach 13 or so, just after they start to menstruate. They will reach their adult height by the age of 18. Boys start to grow a couple of years later but keep growing for a longer period of time. It seems to be because of this longer growth period that men end up taller.

But do men need to be taller?

Biologists argue that women stop growing at an earlier stage so that they can get on with what they are supposed to do: reproduce. It is argued that girls cannot waste energy on growing when this energy is needed to produce children, and that growing and reproducing at the same time would place too many demands on the body's reserves. Montagu has pointed out that, for the first few years after the start of menstruation, girls are rarely fertile, even though they may appear so, and it is at this time that the remainder of their growth occurs. This suggests that we are responding to a history of shorter life expectancy, and that we should reproduce as often and as early as possible. For men, this pressure does not exist and so they can grow for a longer period of time. In addition, anthropologists argue that men need to be taller in order to compete for female partners.

As a result of these biological differences men do tend to be taller than women. In America the average male is five inches taller than the average female. However, improvements in diet and living conditions in the western world have meant that not only are western women frequently taller than men from other areas of the world, but there is also a greater overlap in male and female heights within the same community. Ten per cent of women are taller than 10 per cent of men and 5 per cent of women are taller than the average male.

So tallness means maleness. Even though women can be tall and men can be short, tall things are masculine and short things are dainty and feminine.

This association comes from a biological difference but is also used and perpetuated by social expectations and media images. The media, with phrases such as 'man-size tissues' and 'man-size portions' and images such as 'large cars are for men', promote this association. It is also obvious in our traditional behaviours such as 'a man holds the umbrella over the woman' and 'a man puts his arm around the woman's shoulders'. Princess Di is only half an inch shorter than Prince Charles if she wears flat shoes, yet in the postage stamp commemorating their wedding she has shrunk to such a degree that she looks up into his eyes. Either she was crouching or he was standing on a box!

And as women we promote this idea. Being five foot ten myself I am well aware of the traumas of having shorter boyfriends. I have spent many an evening slouching, walking in the gutter and working out which way the pavement slopes so that I can make myself that little bit shorter. I also know the embarrassment of having a boyfriend put his arm around me, resulting in his left shoulder being wrenched nearly out of its socket. As women, we expect men to be taller, and men perceive this expectation.

At the extreme end of this preoccupation with height, Erving Goffman in his book *Stigma* examined the effects of height on men who are well below average height. He discusses how such men are either excluded from enjoying normal lives or can play the traditional role of short men as 'jesters' or 'favourites of well-to-do ladies'. It has been observed that if short men marry short women the 'mating sequence' is often accelerated, with the dating, engagement and marriage taking less time than usual. Goffman concludes that short people marry short people because they have found an opportunity at last, and because they are expected to do so.

Men worry about their height. It is a weakness in some ways comparable to that of women and their weight, but does it have the same damaging effect on their self-image?

There are certain props available to the man who wants to be taller, such as built-up shoes and tall hats, yet these tend to be regarded as slightly ridiculous. They appear desperate. Unlike weight, which it is possible at least to attempt to change, changing your height is not a physical possibility. Perhaps, because of the absence of feasible alternatives, men simply have to get on with their lives and cope with this disagreeable area of their physical appearance. If the medical profession were to develop a means of adding extra inches or perhaps to suggest that a certain combination of foods would solve the height problem, then maybe men would become more preoccupied with their height, which would develop a more central role in their self-image. The absence of possible change reduces the importance of the problem.

Are there other physical characteristics which are specifically important to men?

A study in 1973 asked a group of men to rank a list of physical characteristics in the order that they felt they were important in determining their physical attractiveness. From a list consisting of characteristics such as chest, body build and face, the men rated hair texture second only to facial complexion. Facial complexion appears to be of significance to men in their teens and early twenties, with the fear of acne and concern about degree of facial hair. However, hair texture and the fear of baldness appear to play a central role in determining body-image.

Baldness occurs in white men more than in any other racial or sexual group. Genes for baldness are carried on the chromosomes of both men and women but require the male sex hormones for activation and for baldness to occur. Whilst white women may show a gradual thinning of their hair, by the time men have reached their early twenties some will show a receding hair line or bald spot, and by the age of 50 up to 60 per cent of men will have lost some hair.

It has been argued that balding is a sign for possible female mates that the balding male is beyond his prime and no longer fit to reproduce. However, this argument seems to be contrary to the rest of male reproductive behaviour and physiology which permits men to reproduce for almost as often and as long as desired. The absence of any obvious biological association between male sexuality and balding has not prevented hair from being central to many men's body image and hair loss being a serious fear.

So where does this fear come from? Why isn't balding simply accepted as a natural response to age or to the influence of hormones?

How many actors can you think of who are balding? How many television personalities accept their thinning hair without resorting to toupees or the 'sweeping syndrome'? The media present masculinity and hair thickness as being inseparable. The only exceptions to this rule are actors (two spring to mind) who are completely bald, suggesting that they have chosen to shave their heads and that if they wanted to they could easily grow it back.

How do men respond to this pressure?

Unlike for height, society offers men several ways to challenge the problem of hair loss. It offers them a way out. Men can wear toupees, sweep their hair across, living in constant fear of high winds, or they can have hair transplants. And some of them do. Some men are severely traumatised when their hair starts to fall out, some see it as the end of their youth and others as the end of their attractiveness.

I interviewed several men, and asked them how important their hair was and whether they were frightened of going bald. I received many responses, all of which indicated that balding was certainly not something to look forward to. Words such as 'horrible' and 'upsetting' were used and 'I'd look stupid' was a common remark.

However, one man did say that he was quite looking forward to going bald. He felt that it was 'cool' and distinguished, although he did add that the chances of his going bald were very slim.

Yet, as with male concerns with weight and height, these problems with balding do not seem to have such a profound effect on body image as weight does with women. This is not to trivialise men's body dissatisfaction or to dismiss their self-criticism, but to put it into perspective compared with the multitude of women who spend their lives preoccupied with weight.

I asked several men if they thought there was a difference between men and women as far as their looks were concerned. Surprisingly many men seemed to be aware of a difference and felt that they were lucky.

One man said: 'Women aren't attracted to men by their looks, they find their personalities attractive, but I am initially attracted to women by their looks, but then everything else becomes more important.'

Another said: 'If you are a man, being fat can give you status and suggests that you are rich and successful enough to eat nice food and drink good wine. If you are a woman, fatness means that you cannot command as much respect, and that you have a problem with food.'

He also said: 'Men's attractiveness is to do with character and personality. Women's attractiveness is far more to do with their physical appearance.'

Another man said: 'Men may not think of themselves as being attractive, or even worry about how attractive they are, but they put their energy into examining how attractive women are. Men's attractiveness can be determined by how attractive their female partner is.'

But are things changing?

Women assume that men get off lightly. However, over the last few years there has been an increase in the number of men used in advertising and an increase in magazines designed specifically for the male reader. Stereotypically good-looking men now advertise milk, cars, food and a multitude of consumables. Men's magazines are full of tall, dark, handsome men modelling clothes and even the male perfume market has taken off. Are we heading for a future of image-obsessed men?

I was interested to find in a recent copy of *Cosmopolitan* an article called 'Cosmo man' which was introduced by the question 'Is he worried stiff about his penis, his stomach, his mother?' Men also seemed to be getting the treatment. The article outlined men's 'touchiest topics' from penis size to balding and described each fear and neurosis in detail. It was sympathetic but subtly ridiculed each male preoccupation. The fears were treated as genuine but not as all that important. The article was interspersed with adverts for clothes modelled by tall men with lots of hair. The jokey article and the adverts presented the perfect combination of messages to develop and perpetuate any male neuroses.

Maybe the advertising world has saturated its use of women. Maybe it has discovered the new world of men's desire to conform to an ideal image. Whatever the reason, men are appearing more and more in the marketing world. And maybe in a few years' time we will start to see the damaging results.

BACK TO THE PRESENT DAY ....

Both men and women have a degree of pressure on them to look a certain way and to conform to the latest ideal image. They are both presented with an ideal body image and yet this image does not seem to influence men's self-image as powerfully as it does women's.

This must be partly related to the fact that there is still less pressure on men, less use of men in advertising, and a greater variety of men used in films and adverts and presented as sex symbols. But it is also a product of how women and men evaluate themselves.

Even though men may feel that they are heavier than they would like to be, this discrepancy between ideal size and actual size is not accompanied by any feelings of dissatisfaction nor does it generalise to self-dislike. Men's weight is separate from their physical attractiveness which is separate from their feelings of self-worth and evaluation of their overall attractiveness.

Women are determined by their looks. Women's identity starts at their appearance. Weight has a great effect on their body image which in turn influences their self-image. Men need to look a certain way, but this does not determine who they are.

Chapter 9

Why continue to diet?

The majority of dieters are not fat, they see themselves as being fat. The majority of dieters do not lose weight, they spend their lives thinking about losing weight. Sometimes they may eat less, but will then compensate by eating more. Sometimes they may lose weight, but will quickly regain it.

All very upsetting.

As a result. . . .

It could be assumed that the average dieter who never lost weight would stop dieting.

It could be assumed that all the negative side effects of dieting would deter women from launching into their next attempt to lose weight.

It could be assumed that the time and energy required constantly to think about what/when/where you eat would make dieting an unacceptable occupation.

It could be assumed that most dieters would soon become disillusioned and that the dieting industry would go bankrupt.

These are all plausible assumptions but are not the reality. Year in year out women pursue their desire to be thinner. As one diet fails the next is started. Leaving a slimming club means rejoining a few months later. Feeling a failure, being fed-up, becoming preoccupied with food and weight are no deterrent to the perpetual dieter. The drive to be thin outweighs any of the undesirable effects of dieting.

But is it just the power of thinness?

Women start to diet because they want to be thinner and because thinness is associated with a multitude of other desirable qualities. Being thin means success, it means control and it means attractiveness. However thin they may be to start with, being thinner is still the goal.

Yet, whether or not they achieve this goal, dieters continue to diet. Dieting takes on a life of its own.

DIETING AS A WAY OF LIFE

For a large number of women dieting becomes a habit. It becomes a pastime and a way of life. Women discuss what food they have eaten today, what they ate yesterday and what they will eat tomorrow. Dieting provides a focus. 'Have you seen the latest copy of . . . . ' 'did you read that slimmer of the year's story in. . . . '. Women diet together, friends can compare notes and exchange ideas. They can go to slimming clubs together, and they can even vomit together.

Slimming clubs often take on the role of social clubs or sports clubs. They provide a place for people to get together, to chat and to make friends. All the members of a slimming club have a common interest and a common goal. The clubs also provide a place to get away from the pressures of family life.

In the western world, families are shrinking and the extended family is no longer so extended. It is easy to become isolated, especially for women at home with children. A slimming club provides the place to get away from the strains of home-life, make new friends and find support. Most members of clubs are women and maybe this reflects not only women's desire for weight loss but also their need for support and friendship from other women.

Women diet because they want to lose weight but they continue to diet because it becomes a way of life, a social activity and a habit.

DIETING AS A MEANS OF CHANGE

Women's lives vary enormously. No two individuals have the same expectations, the same aspirations, the same struggles and the same problems. We all have different backgrounds, different histories and different futures. But we all have things in our lives that we would like to change. This need for change can vary from a niggling wish for a new washing machine to a desire to meet new people to a desperate yearning for a new and more challenging career. And most of us also want to change something about ourselves.

Below is a list of things that people often say about their lives and themselves. They are all to do with change. Some of these changes are more possible than others, some are dreams and others are goals. But they are all important factors in the way we perceive ourselves and our futures.

I wish. . . .
I were rich
I had more friends
I had someone to talk to
I had a partner
I were loved
I did not have a partner
I had a job
I had a better job
I were successful
I had somewhere nice to live
I had more time to myself
I were more attractive
I were more intelligent
People would notice me
My boss would appreciate me
I could stand up for myself
I could control my anger
I were happier
I were more organised
I were thinner

Some of these wishes are to do with changing what happens around us; some of them are to do with changing ourselves; and some of them are an interaction of the two. Most of them involve effort, help, support and a bit of luck to achieve; the rest may feel like impossibilities.

What has this got to do with dieting? Sometimes losing weight may seem to be the only thing in a woman's life which she feels capable of changing.

Imagine waking up on January 1st and deciding on your New Year's resolutions. You decide that this year:

1   I will get promoted.
2   I will find myself a nice new partner.
3   I will broaden my social circle.
4   I will be a nicer person.
5   I will lose weight.

These resolutions, like the wishes above, are all difficult to attain. And to an extent they may feel beyond your control. You might feel 'My boss decides if I get promoted or not' and 'I can't just decide to walk down the road and find a new partner'. But you may feel 'At least I can try and lose weight'.

Women live in a society which is still controlled by men. The average woman earns 63 per cent of the salary of the average man. Most top jobs are occupied by men; occupations such as teachers, nurses and secretaries are still predominantly female whereas lecturers, doctors and company managers are still predominantly male. Women have fewer options open to them. It is difficult to get promoted because it is still assumed that women will leave to have children, that women are not as dedicated to their work and that they are less capable.

As a result of this women feel that their lives are out of their control. They may make decisions about their futures and their lives but the realisation of these decisions is dependent upon society's response. Women may strive to fulfil their potential but are subjected to social norms and expectations which counteract their attempts.

In addition to these social barriers to self-fulfilment, women are not encouraged to understand where their potential lies. Nor are they expected to take control of their lives. Women's role has always been that of the passive receiver of whatever life might throw in their direction. Women are taught to accept and not to challenge whatever happens to them.

Ultimately women feel out of control of their lives.

And dieting offers a means at least to attempt to change something. It presents a way to regain control and to change one disagreeable aspect of life. We all have dreams and goals. If we cannot achieve most of them, at least we can try and change something: our weight.

DIETING TAKES ON A LIFE OF ITS OWN

Dieting becomes a habit and offers change and because of this dieting also takes on a life of its own. Thinness offers success, love, control and stability, and dieting takes on all these qualities. We believe that if we diet we will regain control over our lives. We feel that we are dieting for ourselves and that it is a way to create change when so many aspects of our lives feel unchangeable. A successful diet compensates for other areas in our lives in which success eludes us. And focusing on losing weight compensates for a life without focus.

Dieting is seen as a way to change not only your weight but also your life. Dieting becomes an end in itself rather than a means to an end. Although the initial aim may be to lose weight, the aim becomes to diet. Women continue to diet in the face of failure because even if there is no weight loss, dieting becomes a way of life and a goal within itself. And there is no final goal dictating how thin we should be. The aim is to be thinner. Everyone wants to be thinner. The *process* of getting thinner is what dieting is all about.

Chapter 10

Giving up dieting

We need to give up dieting. We need to stop wanting to be thinner and we need to stop supporting the dieting industry.

It is necessary to realise why you diet and then to find a substitute. Dieting serves a function and this function cannot simply be removed; it needs to be replaced.

WHY DO YOU DIET?

I am unhealthy

Is your weight damaging your health? If it is then maybe you should try and lose weight. But for the majority of dieters this is not the case.

I do not like my body

Most women do not like their bodies. It is very rare that we see ourselves fully naked in a full-length mirror. When we do, we criticise every inch, prod at our flesh with disgust, pull our stomachs in and tighten our bottoms. Or alternatively we dim the lights and walk away.

Overleaf is a questionnaire which highlights how self-critical we are. It deals with every aspect of the body, not just weight, and illustrates that nothing is ever just right. To find out how critical you are, score each bodily part as either too large, too small or just right. There is also another column for you to add in your own criticism such as too hairy, too spotty, too blotchy or whatever you feel is appropriate, since large or small is not always relevant.

I think my . . . . is

				Other
Nose	Too large	Too small	Just right	. . . .
Eyes	Too large	Too small	Just right	. . . .
Mouth	Too large	Too small	Just right	. . . .
Cheeks	Too large	Too small	Just right	. . . .
Hair	Too large	Too small	Just right	. . . .
Shoulders	Too large	Too small	Just right	. . . .
Upper arms	Too large	Too small	Just right	. . . .
Forearms	Too large	Too small	Just right	. . . .
Armpits	Too large	Too small	Just right	. . . .
Hands	Too large	Too small	Just right	. . . .
Fingers	Too large	Too small	Just right	. . . .
Breasts	Too large	Too small	Just right	. . . .
Stomach	Too large	Too small	Just right	. . . .
Bottom	Too large	Too small	Just right	. . . .
Thighs	Too large	Too small	Just right	. . . .
Skin	Too large	Too small	Just right	. . . .
Knees	Too large	Too small	Just right	. . . .
Calves	Too large	Too small	Just right	. . . .
Feet	Too large	Too small	Just right	. . . .
Legs	Too large	Too small	Just right	. . . .
Ankles	Too large	Too small	Just right	. . . .

Are you critical of yourself? How many aspects did you feel were just right? Do you like your body? Do you feel proud of it?

If so many women dislike so much of their bodies, what is left as the right way for a woman's body to be? To whom are we all comparing ourselves? For our bodies to be wrong, there must be a woman out there who has just the right one!

If we diet because we don't like our bodies then we need to learn to accept our bodies and to appreciate what we have. It is only us who criticises us, no-one else notices that your nose is too large or that your bottom droops, unless of course we point out to everyone that our bodies are a problem. Women dislike their bodies and believe that others dislike them as well. Many of the men whom I interviewed in Chapter 8 reported that, even though they would prefer to weigh less, no-one noticed and this wasn't a problem. But women translate their own feelings of body dissatisfaction into a problem which they feel is equally important to everyone else. Their dislike of their bodies is a central component of their identity, which influences their feelings of self-worth.

So how do we learn to love what we have spent so long hating? One of the best ways to like your body is to look at it. The following exercise is helpful.

Get yourself a good full-length mirror. Make sure that it is accurate and that it does not distort your image. Mirrors which make you look larger than you are can be depressing, unless you tell yourself 'I am actually smaller than that'. Mirrors which make you look smaller than you are can be flattering except that you will probably end up telling yourself 'I may look thin but I know I am actually fatter than this'.

Then set the scene. Have a relaxing bath and pamper yourself with nice soap or a new shampoo. Then go into the room with the mirror. It is best to be on your own to start with although doing it with a friend can make it more fun! Have the lights either dimmed or on full depending on whichever makes you happier; your favourite music can add to the scene along with a glass of wine.

Then look at yourself in the mirror. Examine every inch and get used to looking at the parts usually ignored or hidden. First look at your body objectively; examine it as if it were someone else's. If you don't like your stomach, examine it. Do not criticise, but get used to looking and accepting. Thighs are a common area which are conveniently difficult to see. Turn around and watch them as you move. Ask yourself questions such as 'why do I not like my body?' and detach your emotions from it. Try and see it as it actually is.

Then examine yourself subjectively. Notice which parts of your body you are fond of and which parts you dislike. Do certain parts arouse different emotions? Are you proud of some areas but not of others. Focus first on the 'loved parts' and then on the 'unloved parts'. Notice whether there are any actual differences between the two or whether it is just your perception of them.

Repeat this on different days. Notice how your moods affect the way your body looks. We believe the saying 'look good and you will feel good'. But the reverse is also true: 'feel good and you will look good'. When we feel positive our bodies can look perfect and we examine ourselves with pride. If we are upset all we can see are the dimples and loose flesh. This is expressed perfectly by Kathrin Perutz in her book *Beyond the Looking Glass*:

> On a good day I can see dark brown eyes, long lashes, a sensual mouth, smooth skin and an endearing nose. On a bad day these are eclipsed and only the bags under my eyes, wrinkles, kinky hair, fat lips and pug nose are visible. On a terrible day, there's almost nothing to see at all except a blur of indefensible humanity as I avert my gaze. And on a glorious day the beautiful eyes behold me, full of love, humour and intelligence. (p.173)

We need to learn to distinguish between our negative perception of our bodies and the reality. And we should like the reality.

Perhaps even greater than our fear of examining our own bodies is the fear of exposing them to others. Have you ever undressed with the lights off in front of someone else? Or do you lie in bed with your partner making sure your stomach is pulled in and your thighs are hidden? Or maybe you have found that lying in certain positions on the beach is unacceptable?

In Britain we very rarely expose our bodies to others. Most of the year is spent under layers of clothes which disguise and hide a multitude of sins. When we do take our clothes off it tends to be in the privacy of our own home, and only with the very few people we feel confident with. We assume that others will be as critical of our bodies as we are because there is no evidence to suggest otherwise. If no-one ever sees you with no clothes on, how can you know whether they will criticise how you look?

And yet on holiday it is a different matter. Last year I went to the South of France. For the first day or so I lay on the beach looking at my white body which looked in a state of shock at being so exposed. I lay on my back because I look better that way and I put my clothes back on to go for lunch. Then I noticed that I was surrounded by nearly naked people of all shapes and sizes, some wearing perfectly fitting bikinis, others bursting out of theirs, and I stopped worrying. Within a few days I was totally happy. Most people stop caring on holiday. There are too many other things to do and enjoy. And once we have exposed our naked flesh to the critical world and no-one has criticised, collapsed from the shock or laughed, we realise that we are fine, and we can get on with everything else.

But this feeling often goes when we get home. So how do we learn to get used to others seeing our body? The following hints may be helpful.

First, try the exercise described above with someone else. A friend can make it more fun and a partner adds an element of excitement. Compare your bodies and point out to each other which parts you don't like. I remember being at college and getting ready to go out with a group of women friends. As we were all getting dressed one woman suddenly said 'God I hate my nipples, they're so small'. We then all compared bosoms and everyone seemed to have their own personal complaints, but no-one could understand why anyone else was worried. Small nipples turned out to be about the same size as everyone else's, and we all had at least a few hairs growing from them! Women very rarely see other women's bodies unless they are clothed and disguised. It is very easy to believe that you are different from everyone else because there is no-one to compare yourself with. Simple exposure is the easiest way to realise that even the apparently most perfect body is still similar to your own.

Another technique is to try walking around with no clothes on. Get used to watching the television and cooking dinner whilst naked. Don't shy away from communal changing rooms in shops and go swimming in the local public baths.

Learn to feel confident about how you look, and understand other people's reactions to you. If you feel positive about your body others will respond positively. Examine your own reactions to other people. You don't notice everyone else's flab so why should they be so interested in yours?

Oscar Wilde once said 'To love oneself is the beginning of a life-long romance'. As women we need to stop criticising and put our bodies into perspective.

If I were thinner everything would be all right

Dieters diet to become thinner, and being thinner is seen as the way to make life better.

Thinness has many meanings beyond that of simply weighing less. On the following page is a questionnaire to identify what being thin means to you.

Circle the answer that best applies to you.

How often do you think, If I were thinner. . . .

I would be happier	NEVER/SOMETIMES/OFTEN
I would be more attractive	NEVER/SOMETIMES/OFTEN
I would be more popular	NEVER/SOMETIMES/OFTEN
I would be more confident	NEVER/SOMETIMES/OFTEN
I would be better at my job	NEVER/SOMETIMES/OFTEN
I would be more successful	NEVER/SOMETIMES/OFTEN
I would be more outgoing	NEVER/SOMETIMES/OFTEN
I would feel more in control	NEVER/SOMETIMES/OFTEN
I could show the world that I have will-power	NEVER/SOMETIMES/OFTEN
I would feel more assertive	NEVER/SOMETIMES/OFTEN

Score the questions by awarding yourself one point for each
'never', two points for each 'sometimes' and three points for each
'often', then add up all your scores. The highest score possible is
thirty and the lowest is ten.

The questionnaire illustrates how important being thin is, and
how many other changes you expect from thinness other than
simply weighing less. A high score suggests that you expect
many changes.

If you diet because you feel that being thin offers a solution to
many of life's problems, then it is necessary to put being thin into
perspective. If you think that being thinner will change your life,
then challenge these thoughts.

This is difficult because the association between thinness and a
good life is intrinsic to our perception of ourselves. However,
with a degree of effort and dedication it *is* possible to realise how
ridiculous this association is.

The following exercise aims to highlight how it is possible to
dissociate thinness from all the other supposedly related
qualities.

Think of all the things you would be able to achieve or feel if
you could weigh less. To do this, picture yourself as you are at the
moment and then as you would be if you were thinner and try
and evaluate what the difference would be. Make a list of these
differences, and next to each item write down all the possible
reasons why this may not be the case.

Overleaf is a list of some of the possible meanings of being
thinner and a reason why thinness does not have to have this
meaning.

Thinness and attractiveness

We believe that if only we were thinner we would be more attractive. But how thin do we have to be before suddenly becoming attractive? Most women who diet would be considered as thin by everyone else anyway. But they still feel that being thinner would be an advantage. Dieting makes you miserable, preoccupied with food and weight, feel a failure – none of which are attractive qualities. A failed dieter can feel useless and lacking in will-power. Attractiveness is about liking yourself and presenting a likeable person to the outside world. Dieting detracts, not adds, to your attractiveness.

If you do lose weight, will this make you more attractive? What weight will this be, or will you always feel that if only you could be that bit thinner you could be more attractive? Look at the people around you. Are the thinner people more attractive? Do your thinner friends feel more attractive? Attractiveness is about using your body in a positive way and it's about feeling confident with your body. Being thinner does not create this, but your attitude to yourself does.

Thinness and success

Seeing weight loss as the way to success is self-defeating. Trying to diet undermines any feelings of success because weight loss is so difficult. Dieting is associated with feelings of failure which generalise to other areas of your life. Feeling a failure is not the way to succeed. Constant attempts at dieting can contribute to low self-esteem which can actively prevent success. Why spend so much time trying to lose weight, and feeling bad when it does not happen? Success in dieting is very difficult, so why chose weight loss as the area for success?

And if you do lose weight, will you be more successful? Or will you simply be thinner?

Thinness and happiness

We are sold the message that thinness is happiness, so we try to become thin. Whatever size we are to start with we still want to be thinner. But getting thinner is difficult, it is depressing and can be a miserable way of life. If we never achieve the goal of getting thinner, we are constantly disappointed and annoyed with ourselves. Being disappointed and annoyed is not the way to be happy. And even if we achieve the desired weight loss, thin people are no happier than their larger counterparts because thin people still want to be thinner.

Happiness is about liking ourselves and not being constantly critical. It is about feeling positive and in control and proud of what we have to offer. Dieting is about the opposite. Trying to be thin creates a state of constant self-criticism, it is a difficult task and generates a negative view of who we are at the present while focusing on who we could be in the elusive future.

Thinness and control

We believe that 'If only I could control my weight then I would be able to control my life'. But weight naturally controls itself and is regulated around a fairly stable set point. Dieting imposes an unnatural form of control upon something which is self-regulating. Constantly trying to eat less, sometimes succeeding and sometimes overeating, undermines this control and can leave the dieter less in control than she was before she started to diet. In the short term dieting may provide a structure, but in the long term constantly trying to limit your food intake can create chaos. And feeling out of control of your eating can generalise to other areas of your life. Trying to be thin can undermine, not add to, your sense of control.

So if we realise why we diet, and can find a substitute for dieting, we can stop dieting.

LIFE WITHOUT DIETING

So what is life like without dieting?

Imagine not dieting. Picture how you would look and feel. Do you look fat and ugly, and feel unhappy?

Giving up dieting is like giving up an addiction; it is difficult to visualise life without it. Suggesting that people should stop dieting often causes quite strong reactions. In the course of my work I have had numerous people criticise my belief that dieting is self-destructive. I thought I would include several of these comments and illustrate how many of these criticisms are based on the myths surrounding dieting and are not founded in fact.

'It is all right for you to say don't diet, but I would feel happier if I were thinner.' This woman associates dieting with getting thinner, and being thinner with being happier. Firstly, dieting does not make most people thinner most of the time and, secondly, being thinner does not make most people happier.

'You are all right, you're not fat, but I need to keep on dieting.' Firstly, this women assumes that only fat people diet. Women of all shapes and sizes diet, up to 90 per cent of women see themselves as being larger than they want to be; dieting is motivated by perceived size not actual size. Secondly, she believes that if she continues to diet she will lose weight. Dieting involves thinking about losing weight but not necessarily achieving it. It is only necessary to realise how few dieters are successful to understand that dieting is not about weight loss.

'If I didn't diet I'd be enormous.' This women assumes that dieting is preventing a massive weight gain. Some people do manage to limit their food intake continuously and for extended periods of time so that they can keep their weight below their natural set points. If such people returned to eating the volume of food they ate before they started to diet, they probably would gain weight owing to a lowered metabolic rate. However, most dieters are not eating less overall, but fluctuate between episodes of undereating and episodes of overeating. What they are doing is thinking about eating less. In which case, if they stopped dieting they would not gain weight, but would stop being preoccupied with food and feeling miserable.

Giving up dieting is a positive step. Dieting does not make you thinner, happier, in control or successful, so why do it?

What are the benefits of not dieting?

Acceptance

Stopping dieting means you can accept yourself for who you are now, instead of looking to the future for a better person to emerge. It means you can be proud of yourself, and no longer make endless comparisons with better, thinner and more beautiful role models. As Anne Dickson says in her book *The Mirror Within*, that comparison is:

> such an automatic process that we sometimes forget to ask ourselves too big/flat/short, for whom? Having learned the

need for attractive parts, we compare these fragments to external media models, usually without any specific person in mind, and we rate ourselves in fragments and against some internal ideal.

Stop dieting and you can stop making these critical comparisons. The present you becomes important and the discrepancy between that and the future ideal can be forgotten.

Freedom

Stopping dieting means freedom from thinking about, dreaming about and denying food. It means you can go out for dinner when you want and join in wholeheartedly at social occasions. Stopping dieting means eating what the rest of the family eats and no longer cooking two separate meals. It means freedom to fill your time with other things. Time need no longer be taken up with planning diets and reading diet books but can be spent doing all the other things there are to do.

Confidence

Stopping dieting means that you will no longer be faced with disappointment, feelings of failure and depression. You will no longer need to set yourself unattainable goals resulting in guilt and feelings of weakness. Your confidence and self-esteem will grow as you no longer constantly undermine yourself with self-criticism.

Eating behaviour

Your eating behaviour will change. Dieting causes changes in all the factors which contribute to eating. Attempting to eat less creates:

depression which results in eating to feel better;
preoccupation with food resulting in thinking about food and so eating more;
preoccupation with weight causing eating to compensate for no weight loss;
feeling out of control and therefore undereating followed by overeating;

deprivation and increase in the urge to eat;
certain foods becoming treats, becoming more desirable and so
being eaten more.

Dieting aims to result in eating less, but paradoxically can cause
overeating. Giving up dieting takes away this problem. Initially
you may eat as a response to the new-found non-dieting freedom
but gradually food will no longer play a central role in your life.
Stop dieting and you will think about food less. You will eat
when you are hungry, not when your craving for food becomes
too strong to ignore. You will no longer wish for platefuls of cakes
and high calorie foods because knowing that you can eat them
whenever you want stops them from being so attractive.
Cream-cakes every day may seem wonderful on a diet but as a
reality will become boring. Stop dieting and eating will become
less important to you.

Stop dieting and you can get on with life and appreciate all the
other things that there are on offer.

Recommended reading

Brownmiller, S. (1984) *Femininity*, Harmondsworth: Paladin.
Cannon, G. and Einzig, H. (1983) *Dieting Makes you Fat*, London: Sphere.
Daly, D. (1978) *Gyn/Ecology*, London: The Women's Press.
Dickson, A. (1985) *The Mirror Within: A New Look at Sexuality*, London: Quartet.
Gilbert. S. (1988) *The Pathology of Eating*, London: Routledge.
Gilbert, S. (1989) *Tomorrow I'll be Slim: The Psychology of Dieting*, London: Routledge.
Greeves, M. (1989) *Big and Beautiful*, London: Grafton.
Ogden, J. and Wardle, J. (1990) Cognitive and Emotional Responses to Food. *International Journal of Eating Disorders*.
Ogden, J. and Wardle, J. (1990) Control of Eating and Attributional Style. *British Journal of Clinical Psychology*.
Ogden, J. and Wardle, J. (1991) Cognitive, Emotional and Motivational Effects of Dieting. *International Journal of Eating Disorders*.
Orbach, S. (1978) *Fat is a Feminist Issue*, London: Arrow.

Index